#BLACKLIVESMATTER

BELLY FULL

CARIBBEAN FOOD IN THE UK

Words & Photography by Riaz Phillips

Foreword by Wade Lyn

Special Thank You

Mum. Dad. Bob. Aunty Lesley

Andrew Elliman, Dal Bhatia, David de Kock. Ejike Onuchukwu,
Hugo Bax, Ian Mackintosh, Jean Theresa Brown, Joe Weir,
Kara-Jessica Mallett, Maria Paz Mendez Hodes, Marie Mitchell,
Micky Wright, Ollie Olanipekun, Raheema Khan, Robin Clare, Sally
Wardle, Sara El-Dabi, Sasha Salmon, Toby Evans, Yvonne Maxwell

TEZETA PRESS

Supported by:

GIROSCOPE
Turning empty houses into homes

www.giroscope.co.uk

First published 2017
Second Edition 2020
© Tezeta Press Limited
Tezeta.press@gmail.com

Written by Riaz Phillips

Photography by Riaz Phillips

Excl. P.17 "Sam Sams" © Ursula Ackah, P.14 ©
Alan Denney, P.140 courtesy of Buzzrocks,
P.148 © Hannah Hammond, P.207-209 ©
Yvonne Maxwell. P.213 © courtesy of JPC, P.239
© courtesy of Ayannas,

Title and Chapter font by Robin Clare

Art Direction & Design by Kara-Jessica Mallett,
Sara El-Dabi & Riaz Phillips

ISBN 978-0-9956243-2-0

A CIP catalogue record for this book is
available from the British Library

Tezeta Press
www.tezetapress.com
Tezeta.press@gmail.com

This book is printed on FSC certified paper

ST INDIAN
FOOD
AKE AWAY

BARBADOS
GUYANA
St LUCIA
MONTSERRAT
JAMAICA
AFRICA
DOMINICA
TRINEDAD
St VINCENT

BELLY FULL PRESENTS

CONTENTS

BREAKFAST ★ LUNCH ★ DINNER

FOREWORD
Wade Lyn

It's been more than five decades since Jamaican independence and the UK's Caribbean community is stronger than ever, so it always remained a mystery why Caribbean food was such a slow burner to take off especially when we in Britain adopted Thai, Indian, Mexican, Italian, Chinese and Japanese cooking (to name but a few other countries' cuisines) and taken them to our hearts (and more importantly our stomachs).

It was always good to see events like London's Jerk Cookout, and the incomparable Notting Hill Carnival of London, but historically it was still difficult to find a Caribbean restaurant in most of our major cities, let alone some of our smaller towns.

Over the years, London had a fair few Caribbean themed eateries and in my hometown of Birmingham there's a lively and exciting Caribbean scene, but even here for the longest time we only had a few restaurants serving traditional Caribbean food such as ackee and saltfish, curry goat, and jerk chicken.

Almost a decade ago when I visited other areas of the country I found that people could always reel off a list of Indian, Thai or Mexican dishes as long as your arm, but had scarcely heard of these Caribbean dishes. Research from nearly a decade ago revealed that in Yorkshire 51% of people have tried a samosa and 46% a Thai curry, while across the whole country only 13% had tried a Caribbean pattie - the staple snack food of the islands eaten by everyone from Antigua to Barbados.

Not a pastie, a Pattie

You might say I'd love everyone to be eating these as much as possible - after all, I founded a Caribbean food company (Cleone Foods) in Birmingham over two decades ago to bring Caribbean cooking to the UK. I've managed to kick-start the process (we actually sell patties through supermarkets) and carnivals were always a good way to get the whole community behind our culinary culture. After all, Caribbean cooking is all about community, family and good food.

So why the slow take up? Was it the lack of restaurants? Was the Caribbean community not selling itself enough? Perhaps it was a bit of both.

I have considered that some of our dishes can be confusing. Rice & peas doesn't contain garden peas for example but it does contain a variety of beans (peas is a collective term for beans in Jamaica). Curry goat in the UK rarely contains goat meat but often contains mutton or lamb. I realise some people are put off by the thought of eating goat but this is a barrier that they should overcome - the meat is delicious, and also really healthy with a lot less fat than lamb.

So what's changed in the last 10 years? Caribbean food has burst to the forefront of the UK's mainstream culinary scene. The continuous successes of Usain Bolt and the Jamaican athletics team has shone a light on the whole Caribbean and helped re-engage a global audience with what our culture is all about. In addition to this, the advent of Levi Roots on Dragon's Den has made a big impact on the British psyche. With this, a new generation of people have come to understand what Caribbean food is all about. Moreover, from the early days of Notting Hill's modest procession, the bank holiday carnival has ballooned to over 2 million attendees from all over the world all clamouring for a taste of Caribbean food. In cities across the UK such as Birmingham, Bristol, Leeds and Leicester similar patterns can be witnessed with more and more Caribbean culinary events and forums taking place each year.

I never believed there was a lack of eager gastronomes willing to try more of our cuisine and now more than ever it is Caribbean food's time to shine.

Wade Lyn (CBE), Honorary Jamaican Consul for the Midlands is the founder of Cleone Foods, the largest producer of Jamaican patties in Britain. Founded in 1989, under the brand Island Delight, the company now produces up to 9 million patties a year. Coming to Britain from Jamaica at the age of 7, he used his grounding in craft, design & technology from Leeds Polytechnic to launch his own company, seeing a greater market for the patties than his former employer. With an emphasis on doing "the right thing" influenced by his experiences growing up in Jamaica, an emphasis on family, education, training and supporting local has led to Lyn and Clone Foods winning countless business awards over the years.

PRESENTS

FLIGHT OF THE PHOENIX

Introduction

To this day, defining the Caribbean as a whole remains a difficult process as the nuanced differences across each island from soil makeup to tropical climate remain a mystery to those from far afield just as much to native residents. With this, it's possible to challenge the notion of the "Caribbean" and thus "Caribbean food" altogether.

Whilst the umbrella of Caribbean food is vast, over the years in the UK what has been recognized as Caribbean food has largely been shaped by the dominant presence of those descending from the English-speaking Caribbean islands (or West Indies), most notably people of Jamaican heritage. The particularities of this Jamaican heritage began to develop rapidly after independence from Britain in 1962 [1] as the island latched on to cultural means to stoke a national identity.

Historically, with Jamaica being the largest and most populated English speaking Caribbean island providing the most settlers after the Great Wars, for the UK this meant Jamaican norms were the most prevalent on display amongst the island collective.

Given this, due to a lack of knowledge about the distinctions of the Caribbean islands, upon arrival to the UK, many people from other islands such as Antigua and Barbados found they were seen as either "Jamaican," "African" or generally undifferentiated from fellow migrants who may have been from countries over a thousand miles away. Consequently, this arguably affected the way that the cuisine developed in the UK over the years.

However, the basis of the Caribbean spans over 1000 miles that form a grand arc curving from Cuba, just below the USA's Florida, to Trinidad & Tobago just off the coast of Venezuela. Given this vast geographical difference, every island in the Caribbean has a vastly different historic composition stemming from established relationships with colonizing regions, empires and settling native travellers. All this, in addition to inherent geographic location has meant that from island to island, differences in everything from language dialects, ethnicity, and of course cuisine can be found.

From the 15th Century, Spanish, Dutch, French, English, Portuguese, Chinese and Indian (Amerindian) influences all could be located in some form amongst the Caribbean islands. In an article published in 1964, Chinese cooking was said to be characterised by its "unusual sauce combinations," Middle Eastern cooking by its lavish use of olive oil, French cooking by its use of seasoning and Indian cooking by its curry,"[2] and all of this can be observed in Caribbean cooking.

Additionally, the significant forced exodus of an African population via the transatlantic slave trade and the pre-existing indigenous peoples such as the Siboney and Arawak tribes, [3] who descended from Venezuela and the Guianas region [4,5] alongside the later Carib people, (from what is known today as Brazil), all formed together to provide the identity base of the Caribbean today and everything that comes with it.[6]

With such a diverse descendant heritage, so came diverse culinary traditions, practices, norms and food. As suggested, this ethnic hotpot led to what some termed a 'Creolization' of people that lead to an amalgamation of cultural and social identities, [7] which of course included cuisine.[8] Hence why from island to island many differences in cuisine exist. What underlay these differences is a notion of Creole taste shared by black and white, enslaved and free, all giving priority to stimulating spice.[9]

For Trinidad & Tobago, a nation with a substantial Indian-Caribbean heritage and population, the roti (very similar to the Indian chapati flatbread) has become fundamental for Trinidadian outposts as well as pilau rice and rice & peas served with pigeon peas rather than the Jamaican style kidney beans. Meanwhile, for those descending from Barbados, 'Flying Fish' and cassava-based dishes, though declining in relative importance compared to the past, have come to represent their countries.

As another example, in Antigua the national dish of fungie is similar to Italian cornmeal polenta. More so, the native dish 'ducana,' a dumpling formed from a base of coconut and sweet potato, is

BBQ Chicken
Brown Stew
Curry Chicken
Fried Chicken
Jerk Chicken
Fried Fish
Ackee & Salt Fish
Calaloo Steam Fish
Curry Goat, Oxtail
Cowfoot, Stew Beef, Pea's
Lamb Chops
Beverages
Carrot Cake
Sweet Potato Pudding
Banana Cake
Fruit Cake
Porridge

not often found at restaurants founded by those descending from other islands. This brief handful of examples illustrates the differences found from a region often seen as one unit.

Whilst there are many differences, various similarities do however exist in cuisine throughout the island collective. For instance, the manner in which food is traditionally served for a given meal of the day. For an often-savoury breakfast, a hot water based soup often containing, or served with boiled "hard food" such as green banana, yam, or boiled dumplings.

Later in the day, for lunch or dinner, typical dishes of stewed, grilled or boiled meat or fish heavily spiced with ginger, garlic, cinnamon, nutmeg, scotch bonnet or peppers is served with rice, salad and sometimes fried "Hard Food".

What common theme can be observed here throughout the meals of the day is the heavy reliance on starchy foods of vegetable origins and large amounts pulses. With the climate, relatively underdeveloped transport infrastructure and the low economic conditions of the Caribbean throughout modern history there was a natural tendency toward meals that with a fairly minimum effort and relatively low cost, could provide nutritional and daily sustaining meals for large numbers of people. (As an example crops such as the Breadfruit native to the South Pacific were introduced by colonial Britain as an inexpensive and comparatively nutritional way to feed slaves throughout the Caribbean islands.)These were then supplemented with readily available fruits, herbs and spices giving a sweet and spicy accompaniment to most dishes.

These meals were plentiful and often made to last several days – often because of the big families and extended families that all lived under one roof. Where frugality served as a means of acquiring food, that same frugalness was not spared for beauty, colour and aesthetics of the meal where fruit and vegetables were often used to garnish meals. This is most commonly seen on the vivid green and red pickled pepper garnish often accompanying fish dishes.

Given the assimilation of different Caribbean settlers in modern day Britain, Europe and USA being seen as "one" people, and that Jamaica often provided the largest number of transplants, this has meant that fundamentally Jamaican cuisine has taken the mantelpiece of Caribbean cuisine in these western regions.

This is most highly visible with Jamaica's official national dish ackee & saltfish. Ackee, notably, is not actually indigenous to Jamaica but rather to western Africa and saltfish was often imported from Europe. This competed heavily with curried goat (a meal that originated from south Asian curry) and rice & peas (arguably a derivation of the west African dish waakye) for the national dish. Regardless, in addition to jerk chicken, all have become as synonymous with Jamaica as reggae music and have come to represent "Caribbean food."

Although many expatriated Caribbean households now stray from cooking native meals on a very regular basis, the classics are still broken out and demanded at any and every special occasion from birthdays, christenings, weddings and bereavements.

While the composition of each Caribbean nation differs drastically, when trying to understand the food of the region the collective image of the islands is most readily seen at the numerous Caribbean food stops across the UK that all carry these same staples sprinkled and supplemented with homages to the likes of Bajan, Trinidadian and St. Lucian cuisine.

Caribbean food in the UK thus appears to be a collective or assumed identity of the English-speaking Caribbean Islands that have had their foods become the staples and favourites of both Caribbean, English and now an international array of communities in the UK from the West Country all the way north past the peak districts of Yorkshire.

Caribbean Food In The UK

Though black communities have existed in the British Isles for centuries, after the World Wars communities started to settle in higher numbers and a new generation of distinctively Black-British people emerged. The hard times and harsh climates of this new homeland however lead many to become disillusioned with life in Britain. Numerous pieces of fiction and non-fiction literature alike, authors such as Samuel Selven in the novel The Lonely Londoners and Linton Kwesi Johnson's poem It Dread inna England eloquently depict this.

Those congregating in British cities established communities and began building new lives. However, soon came a longing for old familiarities such as the sound of their own music [10] and the taste of their own food. For survival as much as nostalgia, people often held on to what they could of their old lives, largely culture, language and food.[11]

Culture reminiscent of the Caribbean was not readily accessible in early to mid-20th Century Britain. Most vendors did not offer basic Afro-Caribbean produce such as plantain, yams and green banana due to slow transport times. This meant that produce arrived in Britain expired, in bad physical condition, and in any case was too expensive to be imported frequently.

Records suggest that early instances of particularly Caribbean food and drink establishments i.e. cafés, bars and social clubs selling Caribbean cooked meals dates back to the 1920s. This included the likes of the Caribbean Café at 185a Bute Road in Tiger Bay, Cardiff [12] and Florence Mills Social Parlour in 1929 at 50 Carnaby Street in Central London. (Founded by Sam Manning and Amy Ashwood - Political activist, first wife of Marcus Garvey).[13] As described of the intellectual hub, "guests were attracted to the rice n peas West Indian Cuisine."[14]

The British Nationality and Status of Aliens Act 1914 had been in place granting British nationality to ex-servicemen and those born within British Imperial rule. However, Afro-Caribbean communities continued to exist in relatively low numbers until a series of events following the end of WW2. The new British Nationality act in 1948 granted British citizenship to those residing in previous Commonwealth nations.

With employment opportunities broadcast to the Caribbean islands from British industry, in June of 1948, arguably the most famous of the many transatlantic voyages, the S.S. Empire Windrush, costing £24 for a one-way ticket (In 2015 a rough value of £650-£700) arrived in Britain carrying 492 passengers to a media frenzy of front page national headlines.

The USA, which until the 1950s had been the natural outlet for Caribbean migration, instituted the McCarran-Walter Immigration Act of 1952. This limited the amount of people who were allowed to move to the USA from each Caribbean territory to a grand sum of one hundred persons annually.[15] This change reverted the flow of people to the UK, and without this the vivid presence of a distinctly Caribbean community in the UK may not have existed.

The UK convoy carried mostly those descending from Jamaica but also a small number from other islands. Many vessels came bringing highly skilled workers, mainly younger men, who took up employment in London and across Britain's industrial heartland. With this, by the 1960s, [16] the Caribbean population ballooned from a few thousand to nearly a quarter of a million.

This expansion was not without its frictions, as racial tension ensued throughout Britain. Racist social policies and police brutality seemingly exacerbated the situation sparking a number of riots across the country.

In the late 1950s, seeking to create an oasis, Notting Hill Carnival was born. A culmination of events by political activist Claudia Jones, Trinidadian Boscoe Holder and community leader Rhaune Laslett all added to the legacy of today's event.[17] The early years were humble in stature, however over time it became a place to showcase Caribbean culture. Additionally, as one observer noted, by the early 1980s it was "an important commercial venue for the sale of Afro-Caribbean foods as well as drinks..."[18]

With the onset of various outlets starting to cater for Caribbean taste buds, these enterprises not only formed the basis of sustenance but also began to serve as social spaces for communities

MIGRATION
EMPIRE WINDRUSH
LONDON
ST PAULS
CARNIVAL
SAT 6th JULY
2013

Lloyd's Grocers in Harlesden, NW London and R & JJ's West Indian, Dalston, E London in 1982

A number of restaurants have closed since the first edition. Here we celebrate pioneers.

Derrick Blake of Mango Room, London

Rasta Ramses of Ital 'N Vital, N London

Phil Pratt of Scandal, NW London

Marcia Campbell of Marcia's, Sheffield

beyond the living room. Though, as stated, there did exist public spaces for congregation for the Afro-Caribbean diaspora in Britain, these places remained far and few between before the 1960s.

The foreign populace across Britain throughout this period faced discrimination in public spaces of leisure and often found themselves excluded from white-dominated spaces. Hence, entertainment often took place at home with music played on the radiogram [19] and residential spaces were often converted into spaces for gathering combined with the sale of home-prepared food and drink.

In the face of a well-documented employment colour bar leading to severe lack of work opportunities, many Afro-Caribbean individuals who had no real grounding in entrepreneurship saw an opportunity for survival and social necessity. Here, the desire was for places welcoming to outcast communities. This enterprise arguably played a critical role in the economic boost of many post-war derelict areas.[20]

In the 1960s workplace, having to assimilate to English food proved an initial problem for many. In a documented interview with a Ms Edith Stanley, who travelled to the UK on the Windrush voyage recalls, "The canteen food was horrible. West Indians are fussy over their food. We used to take a food flask to work."[21] As supermarkets and local grocers primarily served British and occasionally continental European produce, "Shops did not offer the exotic foods of the islands: dasheens and yams, soursop and mango, salt fish and black-eyed peas." As Edith tells, "You could not get rice, the only rice was for making rice pudding."[22]

As a resident of Manchester, Edith goes on to recount a trend in non-Caribbean business owners of taking heed of the incoming Caribbean population and catering to their necessities.

"Mr Lee had a continental shop on Denmark Road in Moss Side. He was Italian. He started importing our food such as Yam, Sweet Potatoes, Green Bananas, and Rice, Cooking oil. People in England were using lard and dripping. Every Friday evening Mr Lee's shop was full of West Indians buying their groceries...They would meet with other West Indians and talk." [23]

After grocery produce started to flourish in markets like Brixton's Electric Avenue, the first notable wave of eat-in establishments appeared in the late 1960s as the Windrush generation's offspring started to come of age. Places such as Trinidadian-born political activist Frank Crichlow's now closed Mangrove Restaurant on All Saints Road in Notting Hill, West London opened in 1968. Roy Shirley and the Johnson Family's "R & JJ West Indian" on Sandringham Road in Hackney (p.14), East London opened in 1972, Dougie's Hideaway Club and West Indian Restaurant in Archway, North London opened around this time and the Black and White Café in Bristol's St. Pauls area opened in 1971 (with a sister Branch in Brixton, South London opened some years later).

Other places across Britain opened by that generation have become folklore, but for many names such as "Gees" in Soho Road, Birmingham, Delores' in Chapel Town Leeds, Sam Sam's in Manchester, Granny's, originally in Clapton, East London, and the Trinidadian, Hummingbird in Stroud Green, North London lie heavy in the memory of local residents.

The Caribbean newcomers to Britain tended to settle in areas of low unemployment. Therefore, they inevitably gravitated towards the same areas, mainly to London but also to a range of smaller northern cities.[24] where community was arguably more needed. Hence, many of these eateries quickly became the community centres for the disenfranchised groups similar to churches, boxing clubs and youth clubs.

Additionally, where marginalisation had led to organised crime in what became known as "frontline" areas, a selection of these places such as Peggy's Restaurant and later on Broderick's [25] in Brixton served as gathering places. Hence, many Caribbean food and drink establishments that did exist became more than just restaurants and bars but places of cultural importance that linked communities and oftentimes broken and separated families.

The industrial prowess and space afforded in

the West Midlands and north of England saw Birmingham and Manchester become synonymous with mass production of home classics like the Pullman loaf hard "hardo" dough bread and fruit buns. These were produced by the likes of the Davis family bakers in Birmingham, Manchester's Lawford family bakery, Wolverhampton's Oswald and Maureen Young's Hot Bake and the Reid family of Old Trafford Bakery (p.24). In the north of London, the goods of Mr. Patty (p.88) dominated the scene, with South London's fare dominated by D'Bess Bakery. Likewise, in East London the Monero family of St. Lucia gained esteem for their Rainbow Bakery outfit. (p.69)

As transport improved, by the late 1970s, places such as Roy's Butchers in East London's Ridley Road Market, Lloyds Grocers in Harlesden (p.14), Cliffs in Brixton, Miss Henry's Grocery shop in Luton [26] and later Wenty's Tropical Foods in Forest Gate, East London (p.52) took off. These businesses were able to source and import more home-grown foods and products from major Caribbean brands such as Grace Kennedy from across the Atlantic.

Additionally, the interweaving of food and drink with music culture seem profound. As documented, many people began to desire a replication of experiences back home given the trials and tribulations they faced in Britain.

Cooked Caribbean food was often in high demand late at night around the emerging nightclubs, "blues" parties and shebeen-style bars of the time and many people such as Bernard "Roti King" Jackson of Roti Stop (p.166) catered to this. Moreover, places like the Bouncing Ball Club on Peckham High Street in south London was advertised in the reggae section of the NME (New Musical Express) Magazine as having a "Good Bar, plus hot Jamaica Patties...."

Whilst opportunity for bricks and mortar shops still were not an option for many due to financial restrictions, prejudiced loaners and uncooperative landlords, many saw this concentration of Caribbean people late at night as a chance for commerce and served home-cooked food out the back of the cars and vans or forming deals with the clubs and pubs to cook in or around the premises.

Manchester's all-night Afro-Caribbean scene, often known for going until daylight offered this to Moss Side's community with the likes of the Nile, Reno and PSV Club. These places also did well to introduce locals, celebrities and late-shift workers to Caribbean culture as a whole including food.[27] This was a common theme across England at the time with The Four Aces nightclub and Rigley Arms in Dalston, East London, The Beehive in Handsworth, Birmingham and The Globe in West London (p.220) all being documented examples of this.

By the 1980s, Britain's economy experienced a downturn and migration figures far exceeded that of the 1960s, with many more to follow. What was once a community of a few thousand migrants became over one million by 1970. These changes lead to an increase in competition for housing and employment and arguably added to a fuse that sparked many of the racial riots of the era.[28]

Many Afro-Caribbean social hubs like the cafes and restaurants saw themselves routinely targeted by the police and constant hostility eventually led to the closing of places such as the Mangrove Restaurant and the Black and White Café. This apparent purge was accompanied by successive government ploys of compulsory buyouts and rent increases.

Afterwards, as tensions eased by the 1990s (in comparison to earlier years,) the growth in Caribbean commerce increased. The new generation were better placed to straddle social and economic ladders in Britain. Subsequently, as Caribbean music continued to enrapture the youth of Britain, it can be contended that the sound emanating from the islands seemingly opened the doors to many of what Caribbean culture entailed. Furthermore, as interest peaked in music, food soon followed after.

As time progressed, celebrity chefs with Caribbean heritage started to become household names. People such as Rustie Lee, who had a restaurant in Handsworth, Birmingham and Ainsley Harriet. Simultaneously, the pre-prepared packaged goods industry led by the likes of Dounne Alexander of Gramma, Wade Lyn of Cleone Foods (p.4), Oscar McLean of First National Bakery, the Hosein family's Horizon Foods (p.70) amongst others then played a big role in certain Caribbean foodstuffs becoming household names across Britain.

As the first chains of Caribbean eateries emerged such as Take Two, then Gabby's, DJ's (p.117) Peppers and Spice (p.122) in London and later Aunt Sally's in the West Midlands (p.128), with mass producers like Sunrise Bakery (p.44) finding investment to take them to the next level. However, the cuisine still largely remained a retreat for the local Caribbean communities.

Perhaps an arguable lack of business unification with an unwillingness to compromise in taste and texture all assisted in lagging behind the food of other immigrants who arrived in the same era. Caribbean restaurants were for the most part only found in areas that historically had been Afro-Caribbean areas and foods were to be found in small grocery shops or in the "Rest of the World" sections toward the rear of major supermarkets.

Whilst in no way failing to celebrate the overabundance of individuals and families who contributed to pushing Caribbean food culture forward in Britain throughout the years, many claim the cusp of change was brought about when a man named Keith Valentine Graham a.k.a Levi Roots summoned his guitar and began singing a humble melody dedicated to Reggae Reggae sauce (a seasoning for jerk chicken) on the BBC's business investment TV show Dragon's Den.

Many owners of Caribbean establishments mark this as a pivotal moment when national awareness toward Caribbean food increased. Through this, many were able to introduce people to the wealth of other dishes that derive from the islands. In the years that followed some such as Brixton's Negril, Ayanna's (p.284), Rudie's (p.288), and Three Little Birds (p.300) were able to offer a refined modern vision of Caribbean cuisine on a benchmark set many years previous by the retired Derrick Blake's Mango Rooms.

Whilst bigger operations and chains have emerged on the high street, many of the older establishments have, for the most part, remained independent and have almost come to mirror football teams due to the support that locals show their favourites. These, over the years have remained a social hub for nearby barbers, hair salons, transport workers and so on, as well as a place for DJs, promoters, theatre groups and more to promote events and to connect with their communities.

As previously mentioned, the gamut of Caribbean food has been seen as Jamaican, however those hailing from different islands have found their own micro communities. Those from Trinidad & Tobago have found solace at the likes of Roti Joupa (p.150) and Fish, Wings & Ting (p.272) in South London and further afield at Rum Shack (p.260) and Spiced Roots. (p.296) The closely related Guyanese community seek out their Indo-Caribbean favourites at Kaieteur Kitchen (p.176) and Don's Hut. (p.245) Additionally, those from the shores of Barbados have a brilliant representative at Mullins Brasserie (p.265)

Arguments about which shop has the best patties or curry goat mirror home tiffs over which Aunty or Uncle cooks a certain meal the best. What strongly links all these places is in representing a public place free from persecution, a place to see familiar faces who were going through the same distresses, a place to ask "Wagwan!," to not have to feign an English accent, to touch fists, to see "Aunty" or to gossip about anything from bereavements to infidelities back home.

What follows is a brief oral history of just a fraction of Caribbean food establishments across Britain. The selection serves to illustrate not only the diversity of Caribbean communities but also to archive their stories to provide a grounding in understanding for the scores of other similar stories across Britain. - *Riaz Phillips*

References

(1) Higman, B W. *Jamaican Food: History, Biology, Culture.* Jamaica: University of the West Indies Press, 2008. p.2

(2) Ibid., p. 14

(3) Benjamin, F. *Exploring Caribbean Food in Britain.* London: Mantra Lingua, 1988.

(4) Guiana or Guyana is an Amerindian word meaning "Land of many waters" because of the many rivers and creeks, which criss-cross the land. The country is also called the "The Land of six people" because of the multi-racial population.

(5) Wolfe, L. Recipes: *The Cooking of the Caribbean Islands.* London: Macmillan Caribbean, 1985

(6) Lowenthal, David. West Indian Societies. London: London, published for the Institute of Race Relations in collaboration with the American Geographical Society [by] Oxford University Press, 1972.

(7) Garth, Hanna, ed. *Food and Identity in the Caribbean.* London: Bloomsbury USA Academic, 2013.

(8) Ibid.

(9) Higman.

(10) Hebdige, D. *Cut "n" Mix: Culture, Identity and Caribbean Music.* New York: Taylor & Francis, 1987.

(11) Williams, T. The Lonely Londoners - Themes and Meanings. Literary Essentials: African American Literature 2008 20 Aug, 2016.

(12) Cardiff Migration Stories. London: Runnymede Trust, 2012 . Available at http://tinyurl.com/z8fykve

(13) Okokon, S. Black Londoners, 1880-1990. Stroud, Gloucestershire: Sutton Pub., 1998.

(14) Grant, C. Negro with a Hat: The Rise and Fall of Marcus Garvey and His Dream of Mother Africa. London: Vintage, 2009., p. 437

(15) Jones, C. 'The Caribbean community in britain' in Owuso, Kwesi. Black British Culture and Society: A Text Reader. Ed. Kwesi Owusu. New York: Taylor & Francis, 1999, p.50

(16) Ibid.

(17) Busby, M. "The Notting Hill Carnival Has an Unsung Hero – Rhaune Laslett". *The Guardian*, 24 Aug. 2014. Accessed 16 Sept. 2016

(18) Gutzmore, C. *The Notting Hill Carnival.* Marxism Today, August 1982

(19) McMillan, M. "Home Is Where the Art Is." The Guardian. *The Guardian*, 16 Sept. 2009. Web. 16 Sept. 2016

(20) Luthra, M, and Runnymede Trust & Radical Statistics Race Group. Britain's Black Population: V. 3: Social Change, Public Policy and Agenda. 3rd ed. Aldershot: Ashgate Publishing, 1997., p.127

(21) Stanley, E. [(nee Lawrence) 1955, from St. Kitts via Martinique, Southampton (13 days) and later Manchester,] in the portfolio exhibition of the *Windrush Project*, 'How We Came' section

(22) Stanley, J. *Mangoes to Moss Side: Caribbean Migration to Manchester in the 1950s and 1960s,* Manchester: Manchester County Record Office, 1998.

(23) Stanley, E.

(24) Brown, R. Racism and Immigration in Britain. Issue 68 of International Socialism Journal. Autumn 1995

(25) Gordon, M. *From one extreme to another.* London: Tamrae House. 2012

(26) Still in existence as 2016 – Run by extended family

(27) Wertheimer, F. "Recording 1960s Manchester's Buzzing Caribbean Scene." The Guardian. The Guardian, 31 May 2011. Web. 16 Sept. 2016

(28) Black Asian Studies. *20th century history of Asian and black culture in the UK.* 2016. Web. 16 Sept. 2016

[Sun Jam]
"Picka Pow: About", *Reverb Nation*, Accessed 4 Apr. 2017 from http://tinyurl.com/jwdfqoe

[Kool Runnings]
"Life and Style; Jamaican", *The Guardian,* 7 Apr 2007. Accessed 4 Apr 2017 from http://tinyurl.com/k8tft55

[Bluejay Café]
Interview with Joy Blake by Al "Reverend" Thanni, *Art Beget Spirit.* 2019

[Zionly Food Hall]
Graves, H. "The Taste Maker", *Peckham Peculiar.* 3 May 2016. Accessed 18 Aug. 2020

[Bokit'La]
Dancale, J. *Voyage au pays du bokit.* Eds. 2004
Interview with Nicolas Baptise by Yvonne Maxwell. 2020
"Women in Africna History", *UNESCO*

[Mama's Jerk]
"It's welcome home for Mama's Jerk", *Deptford Market Yard*

[The Globe]
Phillips, M. *Notting Hill in the 1960s,* London, Lawrence & Fishart, 1991
"It's Your Colville", *Colville Community Forum*, accessed 4 Apr. 2014 from http://www.colvillecom.com/page/talbot-road

[Rhythm Kitchen]
"Choose Local: Delroy Dixon, Rhythm Kitchen", *Waltham Forest.* 13 Jul. 2020. Accessed Aug. 19 2020

[Three Little Birds]
"'Do what you love' says founder of Three Little Birds restaurant", *MelanMag.* 20 Nov. 2018. Accessed 20 Aug. 2020

[Ireland]
D'Costa, K. "It's True: We're Probably All a Little Irish-Especially in the Caribbean", *Scientific America*, Mar. 17 2015. Accessed 20 Aug. 2020

[Wales]
"Cardiff Migration Stories", *Runnymede Trust.* First Published 2012

Old Trafford Bakery
Old Trafford, Manchester

Like many of his generation, Old Trafford Bakery's founder Wilfred Reid became a known face in his community as a bus driver in the Northwest of England. Due to vast post- war recruitment drives by Britain's transport industry in the Caribbean islands that promised income and stability, this became a sought after vocation for many who had descended from those islands.

Here, with Reid having daily interaction with the growing local Caribbean and African population, he began to gather a community sense that many longed for elements of back home. He found this as many people began to experience the harsh climate of winters "Up North" for the first time and more over the difficulties of assimilating into British life.

In the early to mid 20th century, high costs and prolonged shipping times prevented the level of access to foreign foods enjoyed today. Hence, because of the scarce access to familiar foodstuffs many turned to what they could recreate with readily available items.

As a side hustle whilst still working the buses, Reid, using basic ingredients and experience from working in Jamaica's baking industry was able to recreate a family recipe for hardough (hardo) bread and spiced fruit bun. Soon after, he began selling these two out of his home in Trafford's Clifton Street. Thanks to the growing number of local grocery stores, clubs and shebeens, word about Reid's business soon spread beyond localities of Moss Side and Trafford to nearby Hulme and Longsight. After his house no longer had the capacity to meet demand, Reid was able to find a landlord willing to rent a premises to him in 1960. Over half a century later, the premises still stands in the same place.

Since retiring back to his birthplace of Maroon Town (Brownstown) in Jamaica's St. James parish, the shop has been in the hands of the family including Ms. Thompson, often referred to as Mum or Aunty by regular customers. Thompson, who manages the premises with younger generations of the family remembers the early days of the bakery well. Having moved to Manchester from Maroon Town as a young girl in the 1960s, food from home was very hard to come across. Thompson recalls the nearby Lawford family who also ran a popular Caribbean Bakery from the early 1960s and just a handful of small grocery shops that catered to the community.

In the early days, the bakery was essentially set up for the local Caribbean community and the notable West African community seeking ample replacements for their similar sweet breads. It didn't occur to many that the English population and other adjoining Asian communities might also be enticed by the baked goods. However, with the sweet cinnamon aroma wafting out onto Shrewsbury Road from 5am onward every morning, the produce soon began to capture the attention of all the local residents.

Not content with just selling to walk-in customers who started coming from ever further afield places like Stockport and Bolton, Reid alongside friends and family would travel back and forth across the Peak District pitching their goods to wholesalers and grocers across cities in Yorkshire such as Leeds, Sheffield and Huddersfield. All eventually saw the potential as each of these cities began to have their own emerging black communities.

Over the years, as the production count grew, new equipment afforded meant that they could begin to take advantage of more readily available ingredients and expand their offerings. With this, the shop saw its role in spreading awareness about the swathe of Caribbean goods to those across the growing diverse populace in the area. The walls in the shop throughout the day are lined with fresh hardo bread that help draw customers eyes to the variety of perhaps lesser known items such as bulla cakes made with molasses, spiced with ginger and nutmeg in addition to coco bread and the coconut based Toto bread.

Since taking over from Mr. Reid, the family have carried on the practice of being active in the north of England with their goods found in many restaurants, grocery shops and supermarkets across the expansive region.

Refurbishing the shop in the early 2000s, the only piece of equipment they refused to compromise is the same 7ft English cast-iron oven that too has sat in the same location since day one in 1960. Even if it means sourcing rare replacement parts from dealers. Ms. Thompson explains that this, alongside their vintage (and out of production) mixer and mill give their baked goods a certain character that is hard to come across in today's factory landscape.

Glen's Drive Thru
St. Paul's, Bristol

Since the departure of the Black and White Café in St. Paul's, Bristol - one of the earliest Caribbean dine-in restaurants on record in Britain, there has been a decreasing amount of outposts for Caribbean food within this part of Bristol. Whilst local pubs such as The Criterion and the Prince of Wales have somewhat stepped in to fill the gap, the rear of an old clerical building has become a go-to for many of those in the area. Previously based in the Malcolm X Centre, a place created as a social hub in 1980 from the aftermath of St. Pauls' tumultuous riots, "Glens Kitchen n' Drive-Thru" has provided a place of continuous sustenance for those needing a quick fill from breakfast through to dinner.

Whilst Glen is known across the city for his cheerful spirit, garden coaching sessions and nourishing meals, he's also known far and wide for other talents. "Music is in my blood," he posits. After coming to England in 1967 from Danvers Pen in Jamaica's St Thomas parish, Glen recalls, "I used to travel across the place doing music." As a travelling singer Glen travelled far and wide as a lead vocalist. Those who had their peak clubbing years in that era will remember the stream of names such as The Cue Club (Later the Q Club) owned by the late Wilbert 'Count Suckle' Campbell in central London's Paddington and the Bouncing Ball club in southeast London's Peckham, led by the distinguished, Admiral Ken AKA Big K International. "We had a band called *Romantics* that was formed up in Chorley, Preston (Lancashire) – It was good times."

After the dust settled, Glen returned to Bristol and recalls that he always had an interest in cooking. "I started cooking around 1988, doing catering and such around Bristol." With an open hatch peeking straight into the kitchen, passers by are able to see Glen steadfastly working away, manoeuvring between the several different workstations in the kitchen. Like machine work, Glen moves between the rear sink prepping and washing green bananas, sweet potatoes and yams, kneading dough, attending to his jerk chicken, pouring up cups of his naturally sweet creamy breakfast porridge all the while managing to have a some form of jokes or chitchat with the various heads who poke through the hatch.

Glen's particularly Caribbean take on the English breakfast have proved a hit in the area with his seasoned scrambled eggs a prized addition to any meal and for the outlandish few who cant even make it until 10am without their daily fix of jerk chicken, though Glen doesn't use a steel drum, in any case he prefers oven cooked jerk chicken and prepares it as such. "Trust me! I got these oven trays specially made for chicken!" Glen exclaims.

While none of Glen's food or his own produced drinks like soursop juice - can be accused of performing the supporting role, a star cameo goes to Glen's personal favourite, fried dumplings. Whilst the clusters of pots atop Glen's stove are all near mirror levels of reflection, in the middle an unassuming pot remains almost charcoal in appearance. "Mi Dutchpot!" reveals Glen, a mainstay in most Caribbean kitchens across the world.

Many debate the origins as to why people let their Dutchpot get to such a state. Glen suggests, "It's an old Anansi story," a group of fables that originated from the Ashanti people of present-day Ghana. "Anansi and the Magic Pot." From this fable came the conclusion that it was bad luck to thoroughly scour a Dutchpot though most just instinctively believe it just makes food taste better. Though Glen has two on deck, the more senior is the sole reserve of his fried dumplings. "You have to try one of my tuna dumplings," Glen propositions, "They sell like hot cakes!" Inevitably next on the cards for Glen hopefully is his own dumpling parlour for the world to taste his Pandora's box of dumpling concoctions.

Clarabell's
Bullring Market, Birmingham

A decades old pamphlet for Clara's Tropical Food Store in the Bull Ring market reads, "For a sweet variety of fresh produce; including cassava, yellow yams, Jamaican sweet potatoes, dasheen, cocoa breadfruit, plantain, ginger, pumpkin, eschallot, orchoes, patchot, spinach, thyme, avocado pears, mangoes…Caribbean herbal teas, tinned ackees, Caribbean breads and other tropical produce." While many of these may be common spectacles today, back in the early 1970s when Clarabell May Tomlinson made her first foray into Birmingham's Bull Ring Market between the city's New Street and Moor Street station, it was less so.

Born 1939 in the aptly named Fruitful Vale - Portland, Jamaica, Clarabell was the only one of her five siblings to migrate across the Atlantic from the Caribbean in 1960, then aged 21. Moving to the mainly residential area of Kingstanding in north Birmingham, Clara found employment working in the Bull Ring Market selling ladies undergarments, slips and general fashion wares.

With a number of Afro-Caribbean families such as the Parkers running tropical food stalls in the market throughout the 1970s, as the more senior families behind the stalls began to retire back abroad, many folded up operations and moved on. With Clara working in the market for some years prior and already becoming a popular character, when a close friend Adina "Miss Mack" McKoy moved back to St. Lucia in 1981 she graciously handed over the stall to Clara. As Daughter Stacia, recalls, "It was a very generous gift at the time as stalls were extremely pricey even in those days."

Unfortunately passing away on June 14th 2016, the stall remained, as it has done over the decades in the family with daughter Stacia and granddaughter Adina taking the daily reigns in the frantic market, keeping up the legacy created by Clarabell. Longtime customers recall her persistent friendly spirit, willingness to lend a helping hand to customers and even other stall merchants when facing difficulties. Michael "Bubble" Bryne, old friend and fellow market trader tells, "She was fantastic. She was always smiling, never seen her without a smile on her face, always smiling to everyone she spoke to."

For many non Afro-Caribbean people not highly familiar with the wide range of exotic produce available, Clara was always willing to explain the many nuances of different root plants and fruits and even chop off tiny bits to give a taster. This work ethic and heritage lives on, especially in Adina, who whatever the weather can be seen effortlessly multitasking. At once, scaling and bagging sweet soursops, sugar canes and so forth whilst also efficiently skinning and opening dozens upon dozens of coconut jellies for the numerous punters who have seen the tally of happy customers before them.

As the proclaimed "Queen of Birmingham Markets," the streams of Birmingham residents, including Caribbean TV personality Rustie Lee, who continue to visit the stall have furthered the legacy of Clarabell's stall for some years to come. Moreover, the twenty-six grandchildren and twelve great-grandchildren she left behind, all continuing a part of her energetic spirit will cement this.

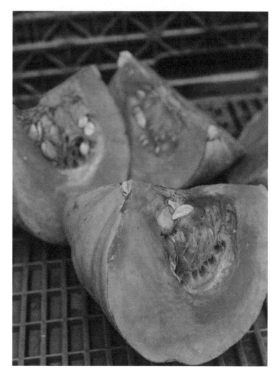

Hawkeye's
High Crown Bakery
Harlesden, NW London

With a distinguished history in the music business that warrants its own entire documentary, Roy "Hawkeye" Forbes-Allen has been at the heart of northwest London's community in some form for over five decades. Propelled by the early success of his Hawkeye Record Store on Harlesden's Craven Park Road, a string of virtuoso manoeuvres and connects in Jamaica saw Hawkeye become a leading name in the international music scene after opening in 1977.

With a Masters in Business Administration (MBA) Hawkeye suggests business always came somewhat naturally and details that his move into the food world, whilst inspired by a love of food also had sound commercial reasoning. "To be honest, I foresaw a shift in the music industry. I saw that changes that were happening." This happened to coincide with a trip to Canada, another country that has for many years had a strong Caribbean community. "I went to Canada in 1985 and I saw how the people there always put their food on display."

Forming the now departed Pepper Pot that now houses Hawkeye's High Crown Bakery in 1985, Hawkeye was sure to implement the style of décor he had observed overseas. "At Pepper Pot we were really the first to put our food all spread out like that in a big glass front. Before that you would just order food and a guy would go to the back and bring it out to you." This deft moved proved a triumph in the area and soon business rocketed and whilst the name has now gone, many of a certain generation still refer to the shop as "Pepper Pot."

Over three decades later, Hawkeye is still active across his food enterprises. The name change came as a way to emphasise the fact that they built a bakery in the rear and moved a lot of the production in house. It was also as a way to incorporate their "Exotic" brand name of foods, principally ackee, callaloo and jerk seasoning from the shop's own farm in Danvers Pen, Jamaica. Hawkeye elaborates, as much as music is part of Hawkeye's makeup, so too is food. "Regardless of the money, this is in my roots. My Grandma had a cookshop in Kingston in the 1940s. My mother, my aunt, everybody worked in the shop. It's in my blood."

As well as owning the first sports shop in Harlesden, aptly named Hawkeye Sportsworld, Hawkeye still found energy to refurbish another of his restaurants not far away in West London's Shepard's Bush called Hot Pot, a throwback of sorts to the old Pepper Pot. Here, under the gaze of tropical pastel artwork, a takeaway doubles up as a more formal dine-in setting where the likes of peppery escovitch fish, cow foot and peppered steak are garnished with hot snacks such as fried saltfish and breadfruit accompanying a simmering of snapper and sliced fish.

Unfortunately for residents of south and east London, a branch may not be headed their way anytime soon. Whatever part of Hawkeye's heart that is left after food, music and business seems reserved for northwest London. "I used even to manage Hawkeye FC". We were the best amateur football team ever!" Records available to the public show that upon joining the regional Spartan league premier division the team won the whole league on their first attempt even despite having three points deducted. "We won everything! Some of those boys went on to play in the big leagues and they were all Harlesden boys!" Fortunately for many of those former players they can now enjoy more of Hawkeye's food than may have been allowed on a footballers diet.

WILLESDEN
HAWKEYE F.C.

WILLESDEN 1984

SEASON 1993 - 1994
PROGRAMME

GROUND :
WEST LONDON STADIUM
DU CANE ROAD. W12.
Tel: 081-749 5505

LONDON SPARTAN LEAGUE
PREMIER DIVISION

SPONSORED BY

SPECIAL THANKS TO OUR KIND SPONSORS AND ALL CONTRIBUTORS TO OUR PROGRAME.

Sunrise Bakery

Smethwick, W Midlands

Few Afro-Caribbean brands have managed to break through the threshold of local grocery stores to mainstream supermarkets over the decades in which those communities have become sizable across Britain. However, a mainstay not just in 'Foods of the World' sections but bread and baked goods sections in general has been the variety of offerings from Birmingham's Sunrise Bakery.

Sunrise Bakery's origins are based firmly in the West Midlands region of England. Formed in 1966 by Mr. Herman Drummond and his business partner William Lamont, the company was founded, like many others, to provide a much-needed food service to the local growing migrant community from the Caribbean islands.

Herman Drummond came to England from eastern Jamaica's Westmoreland parish in the era of the famous Windrush migrant generation. Like many of his compatriots he had an ambition to build a life in order to send for family back home to make the same journey.

With both Drummond and Lamont already established in the bakery trade, the pair decided to depart their employment amongst other reasons in the hope to control their own destiny in life. Starting from a garage the pair had tracked down in Edgbaston, a leafy suburban region south of Birmingham's centre, the pair began the daily painstaking process of creating the soft, sweet hardough bread and ginger based bulla cakes (a snack the bakery suggests is best served with avocado) that they were familiar with back in their home country. Delivering themselves, before building a team of aides, the pair physically went across the Midlands to places like Wolverhampton and the Black Country; Dudley, Wallsall, Sandwell etc., where Caribbean and African communities had grown similar to that of Birmingham.

This continued in popular fashion throughout the 1960s and 1970s until the current director and son of Herman Drummond, Errol, took the reins in the 1980s. The overarching vision of the bakery was always to bring Caribbean cuisine to a wider market. In the early stages of Errol's career where he would often frequent local hotspots such as Bing's Island Hut, Errol recounts, "It was mainly just corner shops we supplied in the very early days, we used to physically go to shops and pitch our bread." Where the likes of Errol and his colleagues differed was the idea of breaching out to a more national level.

Illustrating the change of climate, Errol tells of his forays outside of the midlands. "I remember the days we went to London and we couldn't find any Caribbean to eat!" After the landscape had changed somewhat, the bakery led by Errol had the self-assurance to approach the nation's largest supermarkets. In the past Errol says, "They couldn't see a market for Caribbean food, so it took a couple of years but eventually we got our chance." With their products finding popularity not just at supermarkets in typically Afro-Caribbean areas but much further afield, the bakehouse went from strength to strength, with products now stocked in over 300 stores and supermarkets. This may have been a surprise to many but not to Errol.

With the likes of Caribbean spiced bun and hardough bread established throughout the country, the bakery tasked itself to move ahead and keep innovating with different baked treats. They created Paradise Estates cakes, a process that sees cakes soaked in the famous Wray & Nephew Rum as part of the process and also their new Caketails (a concoction of cake and cocktails) are on the way to a national audience. For two elements as Caribbean in nature as baking and tropical cocktails like rum punch, mojito, piña colada and passion fruit daiquiri it's a mystery it took this long for such a fusion to occur. In jest, Errol suggests, "It's ok for youngsters now, though we might have overdone the rum a tiny bit at our home experiments!"

MC Fresh Bakery

Moss Side, Manchester

Manchester's once notorious Moss Side Area, now incorporated into the Hulme area was a key site of early settlement for migrants coming from what the British once recognised as their colonies in the Caribbean. More so, ever a melting pot of different cultures, for generations, the Moss side locale has been an amalgamation of people from all corners of the globe. Migrants from Southeast Asia, Eastern Europe, Ireland, Africa in addition to the Caribbean islands all found home in this pocket of Manchester and for over three decades Dexter Mcintosh's MC Fresh Takeaway has sat steadfast in the middle of this community.

Here, down Moss Side's Claremont Road, MC Fresh's broadcasted 'Real taste of Jamaica' doesn't just denote the vast array of Jamaican and wider Caribbean dishes on offer but also a Jamaican spin on many of the English classics on offer throughout the day, developed over the years as a way to entice people from all walks of life. These stem from the full English breakfast to the shops incorporation of a full on traditional Chip Shop complete with jumbo sausages, steak and kidney pies and everything else you might expect in a local Chippie.

A side awning seen by those approaching from any direction reads "MC Fresh Takeaway is the only place for the hungry" and with such a diverse menu, you can see the attempts to fulfil this promise. The "Jamaican Fried Chicken and Chips" provides a tangy twist to the student favourite with its assortment of exotic spices however trying to pry out the exact list of ingredients proves a fruitless effort.

This offering seems inspired by the ever encroaching "Chicken shops" that appear to have peppered the local area on a monumental basis compared to the years when MC Fresh first opened its doors to the Moss Side area.

Indicative of many other Caribbean establishments that opened prior to the 1990s, an in-house bakery also sits at the forefront of the shops business. Freshly baked hardo bread, spiced bun and patties prepared in the early hours of the morning provide the shops dominant aroma and are all ready to be served over the counter in the takeaway and also in the adjacent building which is the takeaways own supermarket, wholesale and off license.

As a reflection of an era in the 1980s when subsistence in food was perhaps of more necessity for those with African and Caribbean taste buds, the supermarket is constantly helmed by those with a deep knowledge of the produce on offer – the kind usually reserved for those who've been picking yams and scoping green banana and cassava leaves themselves for decades.

With Manchester City Football Club leaving the area some years ago and as social spots such as the local West Indian Colonials Club begin to decline whilst other local independent places like the Claremont Pub become a scarcity in the city, MC Fresh's humble role as a community hub and forum has increased in importance.

Cariba
Old Trafford, Manchester

In a time passed Ayres Road was a thriving thoroughfare for the residents of Manchester's Old Trafford area. Now, many of the local stores have passed away with the individuals and families behind them or have fallen victim to the shift of passing trade to the city's new shopping hubs in the centre of town. "There's no other shops on the road like this, they've either been knocked through or have been tampered with. This is one of the oldest…That door's over 100 years old!" recounts proprietor Mr. Delroy Tingling.

As a much-regarded face around town, Delroy has an endless archive of tales about Manchester. His shop Cariba, an Aladdin's cave of Afro-Caribbean food and general products, unlike most in the area, has stood the test of time since opening in 1986. Descending from Jamaica, Delroy suggests he was, and continues to understand the intricacies of foreign foods. This doesn't just relate to his fellow nationals but also the vast array of different nationalities that have settled in the locality throughout his tenure.

"The thing with those big supermarkets is they don't understand it," Delroy explains. "They don't know how to store it properly… We eat the stuff so we know how to care for it!" In the shop, above boxes of green banana, yams and plantain, wooden shelves carry an array of jerk seasonings, dried saltfish, curry spices and much more. Naturally, those behind the counter are stocked to the brim with Appleton, Sangsters and vast selection of other wines and spirits from the Caribbean. Local goods are given just as much precedence as famous Caribbean brands with the nearby Old Trafford Bakery (p.24) bread on full display. "Some people come in here and they might only need one pepper, if that's all you need, that's all you need! No need to buy a whole bag full."

With walls lined with island flags, maps and the famous "Jamaica Poster Girl," the shop is now as full to the brim as the 1986 day when Delroy and family moved in. "The shop was full from here to here with paper! It was a coal merchant who owned this building before and it was stacks of invoices – It took three lorry loads to get rid of all of them!"

Describing his family's journey from Jamaica to Manchester, it's apparent that Cariba has always been about more than just a convenience store. "We came straight to Manchester from Jamaica in 1966," Delroy recalls. "My sister delivered the first test tube baby, my brother was a very successful race car driver, he even beat Senna! We sort of made way for others to do things in the community."

"We didn't get advice from anyone, me and my wife, we just started up. I had done 20 years at Dewhurst's butcher shop and got training there. I can cut a full cow!" Hoping to impart this wisdom to the upcoming generation, Delroy articulates, "I always tell the kids, if you want to learn how to start a business come in and I'll show you how to set up your books and everything." For Delroy it's not just about fostering a sense of society in his shop but all over the city, "People always ask - Mr. T can I leave a flyer in here? I say sure put it other there. It's a place of gathering but also like a directory."

Flagging a sense of community spirit, Cariba is not just a place to pick up a quick can of Nourishment or Irish Moss. "In the days when we first came, Jamaicans in general, we would go visit people on Sundays and go look for each other and socialise. Just like my Granddad in Jamaica on a Sunday would sit under the mango tree socialising with all the locals. Now things have changed and there's not many places we can go to." The friendliness of Delroy, wife Marva and their whole family live long in the standing of those who have at any point lived in the area. Cariba have, and fervently continue to help out customers and often go out of their way to source a particular fruit, spice or seasoning - almost anything for a customer if requested.

"We've had people who've moved back to Jamaica and when they come back to visit Manchester they always come back here and sometimes they spend hours here!"

Wenty's Tropical Foods

Forest Gate, E London

Coming from St. Anne's parish in Jamaica to East London at the tender age of nine during the 1960s, it seems young Wentworth, known as Wenty, was intent for a life of enterprise. At a young age Wenty saw a growing Caribbean population in London that was yearning for foods from back home with relatively scarce means of access. With this, Wenty would import sugar cane from the Caribbean and go door to door around his neigbourhood of East London. As transatlantic import became more efficient Wenty was able to source more fruit and vegetables – originally yellow and white yams and plantain to provide to his local Forest Gate area. "Those were the ones that kept the best on the journey, everything else would rot!" Wenty describes.

In the late 1970s and early 1980s word of mouth about Wenty's enterprise rapidly grew throughout the local Caribbean community and captivated English and Asian communities so much so that Wenty was able to procure a brick and mortar establishment in Forest Gate. Here, the original red gold and green banner of Wenty's Tropical Foods has flown high since that time in 1986.

Over time more packaged goods such as saltfish and canned ackee became internationally available and brands such as First National Bakery, known for their Hardough bread and spiced bun started producing Caribbean baked goods in England. With all this, Wenty was able to keep inventory at the shop highly stocked. Quicker shipping times meant that Wenty could sustain a steady stream of variety from his favourite palm-sized non-modified bananas to gargantuan jackfruits. (pictured)

As major supermarkets lagged behind in supplying food for ethnic communities in places like East London or had them relegated to the rear of the shop in "Rest of the World sections," their prominence at Wenty's led him to be held in high esteem. "There are the brands that people are familiar with from back home – that's why they always come back here," adds Wenty.

Laverne, Wenty's daughter, who like most of the family has at some point contributed to the shop over the decades, suggests that what has additionally sustained Wenty's grocery store for all these years in the face of newly opened and expanded supermarkets is the store's existence as a local community centre not just for the local Caribbean populace but for all those who have become acquaintances over the years in the hurriedly changing area.

The space afforded by the shop helped Wenty continue his love of jerking chicken, which he has done perpetually at numerous carnivals across the country for over a quarter of a century. This included the now ceased Sun Splash event, St Paul's Carnival in Bristol, as well as Brockwell Park's annual fair in South London and, "of course" Wenty remarks, Notting Hill Carnival.

Although the shop used to have a hotplate for selling dumplings, fritters and patties out front. The refurbished space round the back of the shop, while discrete in appearance is a frequent stop for breakfast, lunch and dinner for locals in the know. Given his love of cooking it seemed, "a no-brainer," after several years of having the shop, that they should also serve full hot meals such as oxtail, steamed fish, fried fish and hard food since they had all the produce coming into the shop anyway.

Wenty reiterates that his eye for picking out quality fresh foods has been key to his success in the business over all these years, often having to disappoint customers by choosing to not stock certain fresh foods for a period of time if they aren't up to his standards – which at this point can be gathered by from a quick glance or touch and feel.

Dennis' Butchers

Peckham, SE London

Few places in southeast London's Peckham still maintain a sense of community spirit entrenched in an era made famous by TV shows such as Desmond's and Only Fools and Horses. With its unmistakably Jamaican coloured awning flying high on Peckham's High Street, a few minutes spent, inevitably having to queue in Dennis's Butchers, one immediately finds a sense of individuality and belonging that as suggested, has fleeted with some of the past mainstays of Peckham's High Street.

With matching bright white overalls and iconic deep red Puma caps, the team at Dennis' Butchers glide effortlessly between chopping food, weighing, pricing and engaging with regular customers and those who often just pop in to say hello. Working amid shelves containing an array of herbs, spices and numerous multi-coloured signs mixed with the sounds emanating from the radio and the buzz of all the chitchat, the shop oftentimes has the atmosphere of a mini carnival.

Opened in the late 1980s, Dennis' Butcher shop came to fruition almost fortuitously after being enticed to the trade having worked at a local butcher in the area as a young boy for pocket money. After finishing school in the nearby Dulwich locale and relishing the opportunity to get involved in a hands-on craft, his previous experience in the industry and a lineage of southeast London enterprise stemming from his father's shoe-repair shop, all held him in good stead.

Characterising an emerging generation of British-born Caribbean people, with parents disembarking from St. Anns, Jamaica's largest parish, Dennis' family background was representative of Peckham's landscape across the 1980s. This quickly helped the shop become a communal staple for sourcing chicken and lamb cuts, turkey neck, yellow tail snapper fish and, importantly as Dennis emphasises "GOAT" meat not sheep, which other nearby butchers tried to pass off as goat in the early years.

In the time when the shop was first finding its grounding, its main calling point was that many of the pre-existing butchers did not know how to cater for the palates of the Caribbean community. Dennis was able to take the knowledge engrained in his upbringing and knowhow of butchery to give prominence to certain styles of cuts and preparation for timeless meals such as curry and stew chicken whereby almost all the hard work has been done for the customers.

Acting as a provider to businesses in the area such as JB's Soul Food (p.194) and Daphanies plus a number of local schools, the shop has managed to keep a foothold in the area where many others have passed. Although the internet has been slower to engulf Dennis' trade as it has done to many different establishments in the area, members of staff at the shop suggest their ability to personalise and know exactly how each customer likes their cuts after just one transaction will always give them a leg-up.

From the opening of the blinders at 8am until closing there is hardly a block of time that passes without a friendly wave through the window. Moreover, the fact that the team exist on a first name basis with many of the long-standing customers holds testament to a foregone era of manners and respect within the area that Dennis strains to keep alive.

Mixed Blessings Bakery
Camberwell & Tooting, S London

Underneath an arcade awning on Walworth Road - the connector of South London's Camberwell and Elephant & Castle, a remarkable smell gusts out onto the street tempting passers-by and those jumping off a bus at the nearby stop. That aroma comes from Mixed Blessings Bakery. "Specialists in West Indian and English bread" Mixed Blessings has for over two decades become a reliable name synonymous across the country, and especially this corner of South London for baked Caribbean goods. Manning the operations in the Camberwell shop, Devon remarks, "You have to meet my dad! He started Mixed Blessings years and years ago. He works from our other shop in Tooting. The thing is he's quite busy, the only time he has free is in the morning...Early morning, like 5am!"

Without fail, huddled around a stove pot at 5:30am every morning with Rocksteady favourites such as The Hectones thundering out of the radio, Devon's father Lenny and crew start the days with a bowl of hot naturally sweet bulgur porridge, a recipe unchanged since Mixed Blessings' beginnings in 1991.

The crew inside have an efficiency to match the assembly of machinery that fill the rear of the Tooting bakery. This starts with the mixture and milling of the dough that will in a few hours' time become soft spongy loaves of hardough and wholemeal bread. Simultaneously, they begin work on the yellow exterior of their patties that gets run under a machine which evenly distributes the wide range of fillings such as vegetables, salt fish and their own steam fish and okra flavour.

In the early hours before trade opens for the day there is barely any respite in the crew's activity. As one tray leaves the workstation and enters the tall ovens, another one takes its place and so on. As the breads and patties are in process, work on other various sweet treats such as the coconut turnover (pictured next page,) a warm pastry filled with sweet coconut grazing gets underway. As such, when the turnovers make their way to the oven, patties have cooled down and begun to form their flaky outer coats and hardough breads and buns left to rest have risen and doubled in size. As daylight breaks, all begin to make their way to the front of house with hardough bread taking centre stage being placed wall to wall on spaced out wooden slacks. This, Lenny explains, lets all corners of the bread receive a much-needed intake of fresh air.

Lenny's attention to detail and love from repetition in food may have been well suited to a fully-fledged restaurant but he laughs off the notion suggesting, "Nah! Restaurants are too much stress man! I prefer baking!" With this, the shop's minimal but effective approach to producing an overwhelming amount of baked goods and even a maximum of 1,500 patties a day has needed little alteration over these years too. The same techniques that Lenny refined with bread has easily lent itself to an immense list of delights from including plantain tarts, rock cakes, bulla bread, banana nut cakes, coconut cakes and pineapple cakes.

A dedicated approach to baked Jamaican specialties, which poignantly were in influenced by a legacy of British presence in the Caribbean, also saw Mixed Blessings' bread tasted by English royalty in the mid 1990s. Since that time, with the help of son, Devon and daughter, Nat fronting the two stores the bakeries produce can be found in restaurants and supermarkets from local South London neighbourhoods all the way to the North of England.

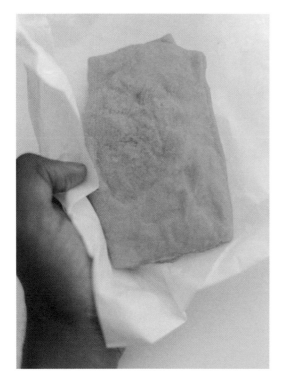

Rainbow Bakery

Dalston, E London

The Monero family have been a culinary institution in East London and the UK for nearly four decades. In a locale where commercial space is now fiercely vied for, the presence of international chains has diluted the presence of the unique family businesses that once lined Kingsland Road. Thankfully, Monero's and their St. Lucian inspired Rainbow Bakery have persevered through this over the years.

Julius Monero, the director of the Bakery explains the roots of the bakery that provided the strong foundation all these years later. With his father, Byron Monero coming to the UK from St. Lucia in 1979 he explains, "My father wanted to open a bakery as baking was one of the many skills he had coming over from St. Lucia. He was initially taught by his dad and developed his baking skills further by working with a few already established Caribbean bakers in the UK."

Realising there was a scarcity of options for Caribbean baked food in an area with a large Caribbean populace Julius describes, "My father first started doing Caribbean food in his first bakery, 'Byron's Family Bakery' in Clapton, Hackney. He opened this location in 1985 and closed it in the mid 1990s. With the support of his partner Maria Polina Monero, Rainbow Bakery was launched in 1987 and Julius has been at the reins since 2003 aged just 23.

For Julius, growing up in the UK, Caribbean food is part of his DNA. He reminisces, "My earliest recollection of Caribbean food in the UK was having it for dinner near enough seven days a week!" Though he adds, this didn't always include the Jamaican mainstays the UK knows today. He tells, "...in fact, those of us in the know, remember fried fish, fried chicken, corned beef. Jamaicans had fried dumpling and other Caribbean countries had what us Lucians called 'Bakes' or 'Johnny Cakes'. This accompanied a nice hot cup of 'Cocoa tea' for breakfast. Another memory was 'Green Fig Salad ' served at family functions in buffets. Lastly a favourite of 'Pig tale soup' and sous similar to the Jamaican 'Red pea soup.'"

This love however, did not automatically translate to the wider UK audience Julius explains. "The local population in the main, back when we opened, were not that attracted to our native baked products. Even up until today, largely they have little knowledge or experience of the authentic breads." Still he finds, as a result of growing international travel people have become more experimental with their cakes, patties and food."

At the bakery the passion for St. Lucia is inescapable with the blue flag raised high in the shop. Julius explains that while the foundations of the foods from different islands are similar there are few things that make a St. Lucian bakery different from a Jamaican bakery. He expounds, "the bread texture although similar is slightly less dense. This is due mainly to the difference in process of creating the 'hardough' and how the dough is milled/refined before moulding and baking. The recipe does differ and you will find the 'Lucian' bread contains a little less sugar."

The selection at Rainbow Bakery is broad with options able to satisfy an array of needs. The plain and plaited soft hardough breads, buns and bread sticks serve those looking for that extra flavour to accompany snacks at home. In addition to this, on a daily basis the bakery produces a staggering amount of fresh goods from their iconic angular patties filled with a variety of meat, fish or vegetables. Those looking for a sweet fix can look to the selection of cakes, coconut infused flaky drops or the opulent coconut turnovers. To wash this all down the shop carries a selection of St. Lucian produced sea moss drink with flavours ranging from ginger, peanut and bois bandé, a Caribbean tree bark spice.

Though Julius' parents opened a third bakery in St Lucia towards the end of the 1980's called Monerkot Bakery (a combination of his parents' family name) they never intended to relinquish what they built in England. The moniker of the bakery, which is a caricature of Byron watches over the shop and as long as that stands the legacy lives on here.

Horizon Foods
Edmonton, N London

Sheldon Hosein, current director of Horizon Foods Bakery, situated in Edmonton, North London recounts a time growing up in London that saw the prevalence of Caribbean food being very much a rarity. "Things were much different back then! The only way to get certain goods was when someone actually went back to the islands." Back then, with the growing landscape of Caribbean food in Britain being dominated by Jamaicans, those descending from Trinidad & Tobago, were often found wanting for their islands own delicacies.

The origins of Horizon Bakery, now the largest producer of the Trinidadian style roti in Britain emerged out of the desire of one family to transplant their home island staple to the other side of the Atlantic. Sheldon jests, "Back in the days when our English mates would come over they'd always end up licking the plates dry," and with this he always had a wider vision that "Trini" (short term for Trinidad & Tobago island natives) food, especially the humble roti could be a hit on the British Isles. This was compounded when a very successful gig with the Trinidadian Embassy turned into a commercial opportunity.

Although Sheldon's mother implored him not to dive into the roti business, the whole family was eventually pulled in when the orders started coming in thick and fast. Very soon, the home operation based out of their kitchen in West London, which had served them well for a brief period in the late 1980s wasn't enough. "We outgrew our kitchen quick and the neighbours would start to wonder what was going on as people used to queue up and down the road to pick up roti from us." Sheldon suggests by any stretch they did not have the perfect roti back then, "This took a lot of changing up here and there but eventually the ladies of the kitchen managed to figure out a taste, texture and appearance" that he proudly claims "cannot be equalled by another."

Needing a "more proper" outfit, in 1991 the family was able to find residency at a factory within East London's Hackney borough, a short walk from the bustling Broadway Market. Here, the bakery was able to upscale the techniques of various different roti and fully develop their offerings. This spanned from the prototypical plain flatbread roti and the dhal puri roti (pictured), a kind containing a mixture of ground split peas with a mixture of spices to the paratha roti more commonly known as the "buss-up shot" roti (pictured next page) for its layered flaky nature that led people to consume it by tearing, or "bussin", it up.

Eventually, after even the Hackney premises couldn't match the bakery's scaling needs, they moved not too far north to Edmonton. Here the bakery sits amongst a variety of craft workshops and production factories that match the diverse fabric of the local North London area. Unfortunately, Horizon isn't open to the public seven days a week, regular mammoth orders from the likes of Turtle Bay and Wrap it Up mean the early part of the week is limited. Between Thursdays and Saturdays however, the regular attendees ensure the bakery's premises is packed out the door. This suggests many had little problem with the lengthened drive to the new location. It's also evident given the amount of people snacking on Horizon's samosa style aloo potato pies or chickpea sandwich doubles with a dash of their tamarind or pepper sauce while they wait.

Furthermore, this loyalty, Sheldon claims is fundamental to how the company has sustained over the last two decades, "We always tried to stay honest to the product, to this day it remains handmade to keep that authenticity and that's what people appreciate."

Tottenham Town Bakery
South Tottenham, N London

"Everyone in our family cooks!" asserts Chris, the man behind Tottenham's White Hart Lane Jerk Centre," a new addition to the rapidly changing commercial face of the North London area. "Grandma always made sure all the males in the family could cook so they couldn't be taken advantage of by the females!"

Under the gaze of White Hart Lane, the stadium for local football team Tottenham Hotspurs, the shop has become a quick stop in for "Spurs" fans feeling the need to dabble in a quick filling of jerk on game day. With the walls lined with years of Spurs' team photos, the wide number of team staff members who also pop in must feel as though the shop is as equally part of their stadium's new facility. "No players have come in yet though, I'm praying for one of them to come in but maybe they're not allowed!"

"Mum would always be cooking and so I started from an early age, I remember standing on a chair to help – I always loved cooking," and this is just so, as Chris comes from a lineage of food activity in North London stretching back decades. His uncle Leroy is head man in charge at the nearby Tottenham Town Jerk Centre and the veteran Tottenham Town Bakery on the nearby West Green Road, a few bus stops away.

Although Chris independently manages the affairs at White Hart Lane he explains "It says Tottenham Town Bakery up on the shop's front sign so people know we are associated with the Bakery in the some way. The name means a lot around here." With customers in the shop recalling tales of Christmas buns dating back to the 1980s, being one of the early Caribbean outposts in this part of North London, for many in the local area, the shop was a common port of call for Caribbean food of the baked kind. With Clarendon-born Leroy taking over proceedings in the mid 1990s the shop expanded beyond just the usual baked goods. Continuing on from the tradition of fresh patties, spiced buns and hardough bread all are baked by Leroy and team on the same original vintage steel equipment right behind a concealment draped with a Menzies National map of Jamaica so customers can refresh themselves on the national anthem and pledge.

From 8am, the warm counter at the bakery top starts to fill with an assortment of sweet to savoury goods including fresh patties and cakes all the way to fried fish and macaroni & cheese that by 11 am has to find more room for the trays emerging for the rear of the shop. For special occasions and catering outings a sighting of the alligator and duck bread so called because of their shapes appearance to the animals - might also occur.

Even a near disastrous event of a roof collapse in 2014 couldn't halt proceedings at the bakery for long and whilst things have somewhat changed in the shop over years, an unassuming bread slicer behind the counter easily predates many of the local kids sneaking out of school for the £3 lunchtime specials.

2 Tone Café

Ball Hill, Coventry

Having worked at Coventry's West Indian Social Club (known for its community events such as ballroom dancing classes) and other Coventry community initiatives for over 40 years, Coventry native Angela and husband Alph were already popular faces around the city. After seeing a handful of Caribbean establishments come and go in the city over the years, the opportunity to inhabit a space in Coventry's popular 2 Tone Village in 2012 soon after its inception, seemed like a stimulating opportunity. The Village, already a communal hub, was a space built to commemorate the importance of Ska music to the city and shine a light on the likes of The Specials, The Selector and other locally based musicians.

Angela, whose family originated in Clarendon, Jamaica, illustrates how she came from a typical Caribbean upbringing, where the females had to cook for their families and, at the young age of 12, was getting to grips with the many different facets of Caribbean and English food. This parallel plays a vast role in the duos' cooking apparent throughout the Café and Restaurant menu. For the Café, this is summed up poignantly with their Jerk Sausage Sandwiches (Sarnies)

Angela remarks, "We used a local Coventry butcher to pioneer our jerk sausage and we thought it would be good to serve them with a side of hardo bread," reminiscent of the timeless sandwiches popular at English café's across the country. After seeing its popularity and following numerous requests from evening diners they succumbed into serving it all day.

Across from The 2 Tone Café, the adjacent homely space doubles up as the Simma Down restaurant between Thursday and Saturday evenings. Here, a multi-coloured menu invites you to enjoy a "taste of the sunshine, good food and good times," and throughout the course of a given day, the husband and wife team strive to provide this. "Our aim is to provide authentic Caribbean cuisine but with the odd twist." Hence, the ackee & saltfish plated with Yorkshire puddings.

As Coventry has less of a Caribbean descending population than the nearby likes of Wolverhampton or Birmingham, Angela finds "If we pair old English classics with our Caribbean classics it's a good way to introduce people to lesser known elements such as mutton and oxtail. Once they are in, they will always look to try something else new. A lot of people around here's first interaction with our food is through cruise holidays or hotel resorts, so it's good to let them know how broad the cuisine can be."

This broadness encompasses the use of the cassava root plant and chayote (also known chocho) vegetable throughout many dishes such as the callaloo & cho cho bake (fried dumpling) and in the steam vegetable offering served up as a side to accompany the extensive variety of curried, jerked and steamed dishes.

With the majority of all food sourced from Coventry, the café and restaurant truly serves as a community affair. Now, although many members of the family are less directly involved it is still very much a family business. Angela's jokes "my mum still comes in on weekends to give a parental watch over and to make sure the ackee is cooked well!"

Healthy Eaters

Brixton, SW London

Healthy Eaters Caribbean restaurant located in the legendary south London enclave of Brixton sits slap bang on the corner of Electric Avenue and Electric Lane overlooking the tenured street market that has been home to a thriving migrant population for decades. The road built in the 1880s was so named as it was the first market street in the country to be lit by electricity. In the post-war period of the mid 20th century, Caribbean people were invited by the British state and crown to help rebuild the economy. They came in droves with high hopes but on arrival things were far from the great opportunity they were sold. Residential and enterprise places were limited and as such they had to concentrate efforts where they could which led to many ending up in Brixton.

Electric Avenue was enshrined in British folklore with Guyanese-born Reggae icon Eddy Grant's song of the same name. The song depicted the tale of a poor man who beholds the things in life he could never achieve and lyrically details oppression from police and residents in the local area. Through this tough environment of South London, a fair few have endeavoured to strive and Stafford Geohagan's Healthy Eaters is a testament of this and also a flag bearer in the local area for Caribbean food and culture.

Where, the local area may have previously had numerous social hubs for the Caribbean population such as clubs and bars like the former 414, many of these have been forced out the area heavily reducing such places for commune. As such, the broad space opened in 2009 that Stafford has evolved to since opening his first stall in the market 2003 is a clear indicator of the need for such spaces especially when they come accompanied with a daily cooked throng of Caribbean eats. The shop's colour motif is black, gold and green showing a clear nod to the Jamaican roots of the shop, however this outpost is clearly a space for all people no matter what walk of life they derive from as long as they are enthusiasts of Caribbean food.

For said enthusiasts this is the place to be. Stafford himself at once can be seen socialising with customers new and old before descending into the open kitchen of Healthy Eaters. While some endeavour to hide their production and cooking process behind closed doors, here the large kitchen is on display to peek into. This is home to an in-house bakery that produces fresh bread, patties (Vegetable and callaloo for vegans. Beef, saltfish, chicken for everyone else) that can for a small additional fee be caressed into the arms of sweet, soft coco bread. These baked goods line the preliminary walls and provide a salivating sensory experience upon stepping into the shop.

Some people only make it this far but if you venture further you'll arrive at the buffet style canteen serving up a plethora of home foods. This ranges from jerk chicken cooked in the kitchen on an industrial level chargrill with overhang on the canopy to capture the smoke from the hot coals. In addition to this oxtail, fried fish and curry goat are all on offer as well as New Zealand lamb chops cooked down in real Jamaican style. These all come with a choice of either rice and peas, boiled rice or hard food consisting of one piece each of yam, banana and boil dumplings. No matter time, the traditional Jamaica breakfast of ackee and saltfish is on offer too.

Over the years, Stafford has cultivated a community centre of sorts with local endeavours always supplementing his businesses. Before the food delivery boom Healthy Eaters had local delivery on Healthy Eater branded bicycles running food out to the wider area. More so, the shop has been an early adopter of an eco-initiative utilising electric vans for its commerce reducing emissions from deliveries of goods and services. Since 2017 Stafford himself has also been a trustee of the nearby Black Cultural Archives, one of the country's premier cultural hubs of Black culture and history. His role here is providing strategic guidance on enterprise opportunities to underpin and grow the continued success of the organisation as well as being caretakers and champions for the African and Caribbean War Memorial in the nearby Windrush Square.

Mister Patty
Harlesden, NW London

Hanging inside the shop, a large reprint of a newspaper article from 1992 shows the front of the Mister Patty shop emblazed with a banner proclaiming, "Celebrating 20 years in Brent – Eat at 1972 Prices…" Standing alongside the then local MP, Mayor and Mayoress of the time is Cindy Fong and a man who rose to prominence across the whole of London in the late 1960s as "Mr. Patty" - Roy Fong. "Patties for 24 pence and Curries for 97 pence," the article reads which immediately hearken back to a time long passed in the annals of history.

Born and raised in Kingston, Jamaica and having come to London in 1960 to join his wife Cindy who had been working as a nurse with the YWCA, Mr. Fong, like many others, longed for a sense of back home given the lack of sun and thick smog emanating from the many flourishing factories in their corner of London.

Seeking to create a Caribbean treat and emulating a French style of soft and flaky patty made prominent by the likes of Bruce's and Tastee's Bakery in Kingston, Jamaica (which had just come to notoriety in 1966,) Roy Fong and family would spend night and day at home in outer London's Sudbury meticulously cooking batches of Patties. Once finished Mr. Fong would simply go door to door in their local northwestern London area, where he had long become acquainted with the Caribbean community.

In a time where even the most basic of foodstuffs reminiscent of back home were not as readily available to buy as they are now, and given the often low economic status of many Caribbean families in Britain, a traditional Caribbean meal with all the trimmings was often reserved for Sundays after Church. With this in mind, Mr. Fong believed that many would find it nice to have a treat during the week and the trade was born.

As common in days before frequent telephone calls let alone the Internet and social media, word rapidly spread on the streets about Mister Patty's enterprise. With newborn children in the house, the scale had become too unsustainable to continue in a household residence and Mr. Patty was able to secure a shop in Roundwood Road, which lies between Willesden and the Harlesden area of northwest London.

Given its proximity to venues such as the Apollo Club, the shop became a pit stop to many of the travelling "packages" of artists who would be sent over to tour Britain from the Americas and Caribbean. Here, over the decades, Mister Patty entrenched its place in local folklore. Since his untimely passing in 2012, the reigns of the shop have been in hands of Mr. Patty's son Rog, who tirelessly handles every element of the business where the shop's second incarnation has existed since 1986. Whilst Cindy has since retired to the quieter outer regions of London, as a veteran staunch businesswomen and local advocate she reassures, "Even now I still have ideas and want to do things!"

The shop is adorned with an original Island Designs Jamaica map - a visual mainstay of many Jamaican businesses and households accompanied by maps of Grenada, Barbados and signed records from many of the famed music artists who have had a munch of Mister Patty's signature item. With this, the shop acts here as a monument of cultural history on a rapidly changing Craven Park Road.

Many of the elder customers who visit the shop often recount tales of the old days when Mister Patty was a highly visible character amongst the streets of northwest London and how things used to be "Back then" whilst making sure to acknowledge Mister Patty's role as an originator in Caribbean food culture in Britain.

MISTER PATTY

A GREAT NAME IN AFRO WEST INDIAN FOOD

965 4055

CELEBRATING 20 YEARS IN BRENT
EAT AT 1972 PRICES ON THE 27th MAY

Bushman Kitchen

Brixton Station Rd, SW London

A pillar of the local community, Earl "Bushman" Brown, often referred to as "Daddy Bush" around the streets of Brixton perhaps as his kitchen which has been active since the late 1980s is now older than many of its frequent customers. The origins of the Bushman name come from a popular tag used in Jamaica and other Caribbean islands for those known around town for selling teas and other nutritional and healing herbs such as Chaney root, Irish moss and sorrel.

Growing up in South London, with his family having descended from Jamaica, Bushman steadily built up a reputation for himself in this trade and when the opportunity arose to combine this life backdrop with a fully-fledged kitchen in the Brixton area he immediately leapt at the chance. Once the word got out about Bushman's wholesome hearty hot food swiftly available throughout the course of the working day, Bushman's name spread further afield in London.

A snug partition beneath the staircase leading to Brixton's Recreational Centre on Brixton Station Road, amongst the sprawling street market and bustle of the vibrant Brixton Village lies the kitchen. Here, after a long day's work, Bushman can be seen perched outside explaining the intricacies of Caribbean food to first timers who've been told about his shop or engaging in deep chat with dozens of his friends who come by to check for him every day.

There are barely any leftovers at the Kitchen as nothing remains at the end of the day. At the height of lunch the queues snake far outside of the shop. "You should have seen it during Brixton Splash!" (The now defunct street party in the area.) Bushman gleefully exclaims, "The queue was all the way down there!" – pointing to the cross-section of the nearby Brixton Road. In addition to this, Bushman himself routinely distributes all leftovers to those in need in the local area.

Given this attitude and the volume of ingredients needed to supply these hungry mouths each day, Bushman is up at 5am daily, sourcing meat and vegetables from the local Brixton market stalls in order to cook every offering fresh from scratch. By 7am time is spent preparing fresh juices, kneading dough for dumplings and festivals before he is joined by his son Joe and the rest of the crew to prepare all the food before the inevitable daily queue emerges.

When asked how he has been able to keep serving for over a quarter of a century and attend the Notting Hill Carnival in high spirits without fail every year, the secret he proclaims, "It's the Moringa seeds!" Eating these everyday alongside a powerful shot of herbal bitters helps the digestive system and, "Keeps you strong!" Bushman educates. If you're lucky (or unlucky) the crew may merrily offer you a bitter shot with your meal.

R&B
Lower Clapton, E London

Where Hackney's Mare Street begins to creep into Lower Clapton in the east end of London, R&B Caribbean Takeaway has virtually served as the neighbourhood's kitchen and dining room, especially for residents of the opposite Pembury Estate, since the late 1980s. In the face of vast change, not only in the shop, but the entire area in general, one resolute constant over that quarter of a century has been Paulette Wilsow known throughout the area as Mrs. Bev.

Mrs. Bev, The B in R&B, who started as a cook "Many moons ago" as she puts it has since become co-owner of the establishment with partner Roan, the R in R&B, an expatriate of St. James, Jamaica. Coming to South London in her younger years from Jamaica's capital of Kingston, Bev recalls her early days in Brixton, "There were plenty of Caribbean shops back then in those days." With a fine talent for cooking big quantities for large numbers of people, Bev rapidly became known for her culinary skills in the local area. Having then decided to make a move north of the river from Brixton to Hackney, she carried this with her to the location on Clarence road where the shop remains today.

A daily 5:30-6:00am start sees the preparation of peppered prawns, sprats and many other staples that are all chalked onto the lofty blackboard by the near front window. The jam-packed menu at R&B that helps salivate passers-by exemplifies Bev's delight in cooking a variety of dishes throughout the week such as her famed BBQ wings and red pea soup. As she puts

it, "Everything is a favourite!" Fridays are savoured for a rarity of R&B's specialty curried crab and weekends for fish dishes such as stewed and roasted snapper.

Today Mrs Bev's still name rings bells as far as South London, as do her library of recipes. She also spent some time lending her expertise teaching Control Tower (p.98) her own recipe for festivals, which have a golden glow in the shop's display.

Although much of the prep is done in the early hours of the day, certain pieces such as the oven-top grilled breadfruit are done throughout the day to ensure absolute freshness and texture in taste. The pair also partition time to their Natural Choice Juices utilising the many nearby worldly markets throughout East London, experimenting with any particular ingredients that take their fancy. Sweet and milky sour-sop juice, pineapple, guava and carrot all don the shop's fridges. Roan also proudly exhibits his green juice as a way of providing healthier options for the people of Hackney, "Its got lettuce, cucumber, celery, ginger, lemon, carrot and a lickle something extra!"

With the solitary chairs in the front section of R&B always occupied by locals recanting old stories and the sliding floor-to-ceiling frontage often turning into a front porch. Whatever the weather, many choose to congregate in the shop's rear seating area kitted with an almost 10ft dub sound system. R&B has been and still is a vibrant destination for the long-standing community to come together and socialise.

R & B CARIBBEAN

JERK CHICKEN

R&B RESTURANT
Pepper Prawn
Rice & Peas
Plain Rice
Hard Food
Curry goat
Curry Chicken
Stew Chicken
Jerk Chicken
Fried Chicken
Ackee & Saltfish
Butter Bean & Saltfish
Callaloo & Saltfish
Liver
Oxtail & Bean
Fry Saltfish
Fried Fish
Stew
B.B.Q Chicken
Dumplings

Patties
Cake
Porridage
Tea
Mint Tea
Coffee
Chocolate Tea
Festival
Fried Dumplin
Mix Veg
Fry Plantain
Fried Breadfruit
Salad

Soup
Red Pea soup
Chicken Soup
Fish Tea
Goat Soup

Control Tower

Coldharbour Lane, SW London

On the 1977 record "Rasta Ambassador," prolific Jamaican recording artist U-Roy emotionally sang, "Ain't no war in the Ghetto," preaching, "Peace and Love to all mankind, from the youth to the Grown-ups," on the album's opening track entitled Control Tower.

This was a much-needed decree given the turbulence in southwest London soon after in the early 1980s following numerous tensions that eventually culminated in the devastating 1981 Brixton Riots. In the aftermath of this, similar sentiment has underlined the foundation of the area's long-standing Caribbean takeaway, Control Tower, which since 1989 has sat adjacent to the unmistakable Red, Gold and Green - Ackee Tree Taxi service almost half way between Camberwell and Brixton.

After being greeted by a large golden-framed portrait of the historic Emperor of Ethiopia, Haile Selassie, you might find DP, Mrs. Rasta or one the other tenured crew members nestled in the corner of the yellow-beamed enclosure amongst a collection of Djembe Drums and Evergreen plants. In this enclosure, each takes shifts cooking up produce at any time of day given the shop's 24-hour operation.

This around-the-clock service proved a hit in the early days, particularly with the nearby taxi drivers who frequently worked around the clock and also the local transport operators and general tradesmen who often worked "graveyard" shifts deep into the night.

Alongside those working at nearby bus depots these people would often miss the fare of other nearby food stops that had already closed for the day. The late openings also meant that for those of the previously mentioned occupations who didn't derive from Caribbean descent the Control Tower was their first foray into the food of the islands, as the shop was the only place to get a full homely meal in the small hours of night.

The current team has been holding down the fort at Control Tower for some years now since founder and long-time resident of the area Mr. J. Parker, a native of St. Elizabeth, Jamaica established it. Around the clock jerk chicken, escovitch fish, fried dumplings and plantain emerge from the oven and lie in wait on the display counter. As a relatively early participant in South London's Caribbean food scene, Control Tower has served as a training ground for many other aspiring cooks who have gone on to work and own several establishments around London.

Additionally, over the years the establishment has also become, as was intended, a place for the distribution of cultural knowledge for Caribbean, Rastafarian and African heritage. This happens mainly through the sale of Ethiopian calendars and other African-based memorabilia and pamphlets but it may often just be in the form of a chat with the team and streams of people who come through doors every day.

Russell's

Lozells Road, Birmingham

More than two decades ago, before the notion of "farm-to-table" dining had become a common trend in the food world, Mr. Roy Johnson had a vision of owning a farm in Jamaica from which he could send the produce across the Atlantic to his corner of England's second city, Birmingham.

With this, he would be able to provide a variety of fresh tropical goods for the area's burgeoning diverse community. All this, whilst cultivating value and growth back home on the island. Acting on this dream, the early 1990s saw the birth of Russell's in Birmingham's renowned "Lozells" area, named after the Lozell's Road that runs through it.

The business is an octopus of an institution with various arms. The most prominent being a large supermarket, a day-long canteen and takeaway post known locally for its salt beef snacks and patties. The genesis of Russell's however, like many other longstanding Caribbean institutions had very humble beginnings with Mr. Johnson making bread from a small unit not too far away in the Saltley area for the local community. As trade increased, Johnson and friends needed a bigger space to produce bread and after some searching found home in a shoe manufacturer's workshop that had unfortunately had met its fate in a fire during the riots that ravaged parts of the Handsworth area during the mid-1980s.

To upscale the bread production and to diversify the baked offerings to include the likes of Russell's popular "Rasta Buns," Johnson travelled across the continent eventually sourcing an assembly of machinery in Spain and shipping it back to England. "It was hard to find that kind of machinery here in England so you had to travel but it was worth because in them days machines were really built to last," contends current manager Young Roy, who now oversees duties at the complex with Mr. Johnson more frequently back home tending to the twenty acre farm in Linstead, Jamaica. "The farm has sweet potatoes, yams, ackee, sugar cane, jelly nuts, coconuts and herbs like thyme" explains Young Roy.

The front of the store also houses curiosities such as dried scotch bonnet, gum Arabic used for stabilising food and "ramgoat da shalong" (damiana plant) used in tea and a variety of health remedies. "The idea was that nothing should go to waste once it's over here so if we see that yams in the supermarket aren't selling one day we'll put them straight into a stew and let the customers next door know there's a special on."

This notion of versatility was inspired by several of Mr. Johnson's early spells in London, especially North London where he saw how some of the new communities there were sustaining themselves. Following this, Russell's experienced a natural progression as they acquired the neighbouring spaces and aimed to internalise every aspect of their commerce. They added a butchers at the rear of the supermarket, shifting the bakery out of sight, having the canteen and created their own products like the almond and rose water concoction for cakes, cordial syrups for drinks and making dry and wet seasonings. All these are self made and monitored by Russell's so they can personally manage and lower the content of additives that Young Roy suggests is rife in mainstream foodstuffs.

"The idea was always to build something for the whole community – it didn't matter where you came from in the world Russell's could be a peaceful community centre – You see it now, people come here and they meet people they haven't seen in years!" Spending some time in the canteen, with its vast menu of Caribbean favourites like curry goat, saltfish and sea bream this is apparent.

With the variety of local vendors in the region Russell's is more than happy to extend its premises as a physical space to reach the community. This includes anything from upstart health drink specialists to the likes of ConsciousPrints whose posters on a plethora of diet information, healthy living and African education line the walls of the Canteen. As Young Roy puts it, "A one stop shop for the community."

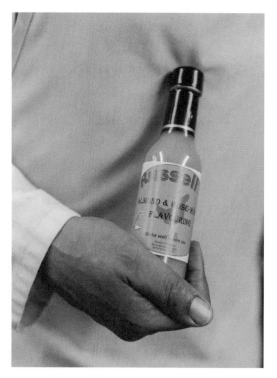

Dougy's Caribbean Delicatessen

Moss Side, Manchester

Down Great Western Street, a passage that links two of Greater Manchester's main roads - Oxford Road and Princess Road, you'll find Dougie's Caribbean Delicatessen, which since relocating to the city's Moss Side area, came to be a runaway success not just locally but further afield, with the name carrying high regard all the way from Liverpool, Sheffield and everywhere in between.

"My vision was to improve service, guarantee quality, consistency under the motto - where quantity counts but quality matters," remarks Manchester-native Denis Douglas. This points to a key reason his shop has found so much favour both across the Northwest and in many online forums like Tripadvisor where the shop ranks in the city's elite echelon, not just for Caribbean food institutions but all food establishments in general.

Coming from a highly regarded family in the community helped kick-start the engine in 1990, when Denis and his older brother set up a Caribbean grocery shop in the Old Trafford area. "We used to sell yams, bananas, everything – but my brother (who now runs two restaurants in Mandeville, Jamaica) thought it would be better if we actually cooked the food we had instead." After some initial cooking expertise via consultation with Mama Dougy (who now can often be found first in the kitchen at half seven each morning) the business instantly took off.

Having relocated around Manchester through the years, the business eventually settled in its current Moss Side location in the place of the former Alvino's. Having taken a more dominant role in the business in 2009, Denis was very keen to "bring the business into the 21st Century," and was very keen on stressing the "delicatessen" component in the shop's title, drawing on influences from his West Indian and South American family in conjunction with inspiration from his worldly travels experiencing a certain cadence of service at cafés and bistros. This is fervently poured back into the shop's diverse menu, which informs Dougy's catchphrase "Come taste the flavour!" As Denis attests, "We're trying to reach out to as many people as possible – so when we do our food we have to think of everyone's palette without losing the quality or the taste and flavour."

"Everybody does jerk chicken different – that's why we call it Dougy's Jerk not authentic jerk, though some people like it on the jerk pan, we don't do ours on the jerk pan, we bake ours, we use low fat oils – we try and deal with a lot of the health issues that are prevalent in the area." This level of thought is perhaps what has attracted numerous local footballers and celebrities over years. Meanwhile, the free samples of aloe vera and pomegranate slushies may be what has the local schoolkids rushing in day after day. "Ours is home style cooking... My mum's home style cooking and that's what the people like."

Denis pays reverence to the changing face of this corner of Manchester. "Back in the early days it was mainly Caribbeans, Asians and English but now we have Eastern Europeans and East Africans for example, it's so much more multicultural now." Dougy elucidates a notion of versatility that he strains to keep in the business. "We do jerk lamb chops, we incorporate the likes of fufu and garri in our menu which is a treat for the West African community while on Sundays we do a proper English roast with all the trimmings - Yorkshire puddings, roast potatoes, you name it." As Denis marvels, "We always sell out on Sundays, we even have people ringing up on Thursdays to reserve a meal! It's just us being creative and embracing the whole community."

Not content with just cooking, Dougy's also has its own in-house bakery that has assisted in reducing costs and allowed Dougy's to sell patties for 99p, "The cheapest in all of Manchester," alongside a slate of mouth-watering deserts such as the banana cake, cornflake tart (pictured next page) and apple crumble.

The same premises also houses a school and education centre created by Denis' sister. With numerous awards from the likes of the NSPCC, Bernardos and New Children's hospital, this type of charitable outreach perfectly illustrates the youth and community outreach done by the family and has shaped Dougy's into becoming much more than just a food stop over the years.

Cummin' Up
Brighton & SE London

With an encyclopaedic memory regarding who's who in the world of Britain's Caribbean culinary scene, for over two decades Richard Simpson has been at the heart of the scenes progression. As a young man about town in his native South London, his rousing youth provided the backdrop for his prosperous catering business and chain of takeaways and restaurants - Cummin' Up.

A familiar face out and around South London, Richard recalls at an early age, "I was a hustler from young! Me and my friends used to do loads of little things to get by. There was Penny for the Guy, that was when you had a Guy Fawkes dummy and would go around asking for change to get fireworks for Bonfire Night." Richard adds, "We use to watch (look after) cars too. For those who came to watch the dogs at the old Catford race track and we all had our own patches outside the stadium." A reminiscing Richard tells, "That was good for a while!" until an unfortunate event with an exotic car he was watching put that livelihood on hold. "I did it all. I worked in Lewisham McDonalds part-time when I was a teen."

Following a career in the engineering sector, Richard's attention turned to the food world in the late 1980s. He saw a discrepancy between places to get a flavoursome meal and the growing Caribbean community alongside streams of hungry art students. This was a time when South London's New Cross was equally eccentric but not as yet developed as it has come to be over years. Richard jumped on an opportunity there that presented itself where, since opening its doors in 1991, the shop remains today. "I noticed all the people coming from the railway station and there was nowhere close for them to grab a quick bite to eat on the way in or out."

With a comprehension of the local area to rival the London Black Cab Knowledge, after the New Cross shop took off, ventures nearby in Catford and Sydenham were followed with equal esteem. Given this, local regulars may not be aware that Richard also has a chain down in England's lively city of Brighton.

"From some years back they had what they called the Alternative Notting Hill Carnival, outside the Concorde venue on the beachfront and someone suggested I should get involved and it worked really well." It went so well it seems that people from the venue started to get a bit worried. "Our 20ft trailer nearly didn't make it though, I nearly skidded off the motorway coming down to Brighton. After that worked it was like a lightbulb went off." Subsequently locating a spot in Brighton's Preston circus Richard expanded his operation.

With South London's Catford premises having a total renovation, the new dine-in menu pioneered by Richard's daughter suggests the direction Cummin' Up is moving toward. With each table decorated with informing placards of Caribbean cuisine from the different islands, an emphasis has and continues to be placed on drawing inspiration not just from Jamaica but across the whole Atlantic isles.

Caribbean versions of gourmet burgers, tortillas and a wide selection of "Grandma Toots" deserts including a deluxe red velvet cake take centre stage during the week, whilst Sundays in Catford are reserved for the all you can eat buffet. Stressing a desire for "consistency in flavour and taste," the buffet offers a wealth of Cummin' Up classics found at the Brighton and New Cross shops that have been refined over the years since 1991. Curried goat, oxtail, stewed chicken, steamed fish and more fill the hot trays to the brim until finish.

With community outreach being a pillar of Cummin' Up, when not found in one of the shops or catering a private event, Richard and team can often be located at a myriad of local communal events using the shop's food and name to lend a helping hand. A look at the signage of the Brighton shop reads, "Bakery, Caterers, Takeaway and Cultural Center." To Richard, the latter of the list is the most important. Stretching the Cummin' Up name as far as Grenada, the shop represents over a quarter of a century in building a bridge between all walks of life.

Sun Jam
Woolwich, SE London

Sitting off a quiet side street, a few minutes walk from the Woolwich Arsenal and a short stride from the River Thames, the bold yellow motif of Sun Jam Caribbean Takeaway helps it live up to its name and provide a splash of colour to Spray Street where, since its creation in 1992 the shop has endured the test of time.

Founded by by music artist Picka Pow (the name of a common dice game in Jamaica) as an extension of his Sun Jam record label. As a native of Southeast London, the early days of Pow's career saw him collaborating with England's Jah Shaka Soundsystem and the infamous Sugar Minott's Youth Promotion crew in Jamaica. Working across many of Jamaica's most prominent music studios, such as King Tubby's studio, Buju Banton's Cell Block Studio and Donovan Germain's Penthouse Records Studio, amongst a slew of others.

Given this experience, Picka Pow's grounding in the music industry was more than sufficient to form his own record label Sun Jam records in 1985, performing shows across Europe and the Americas and collaborating with artists such as Top cat, Rick Wayne, Lloydie Roots, Don Ranger and Earl Sixteen to name but a few from the immense who's who of talent across the reggae scene.

As documented, when reggae influenced sounds started to become less relevant to the youth of the Caribbean diaspora, which coincided with an overall downturn in the music industry as a whole, Mr Pow's focus turned toward providing a place of sustenance for the community of Woolwich, a place on the outer limits of southeastern London, which has for some years had a notable Caribbean community and since the late 1990s an ever present array of people descending from West Africa. "I had an idea and it worked," describes Pow, "The whole thing just took off."

With the team prepping and serving popular Caribbean eats from hot banana and cornmeal porridges, meat and Ital soups to jerk and curry chicken plus a wide variety of fish dishes throughout its eleven-hour service, Sun Jam's humble space can go from quiet to spontaneously chock-full of eager mouths at any time of day.

"You can feel the vibes!" Picka declares. Given the shop's roots in a passion for music, the speakerbox and sound system placed outside the shop every day (as it has been for many years) ensures the legacy of the Sun Jam sound and reggae influenced culture as a whole will live on for some years to come, both inside the shop and outside in this pocket of London.

DJ's
Harrow Road, W London

On the same road as St. Mary's Cemetery, resting place of Nurse Mary Seacole, a prominent nurse and humanitarian of Jamaican descent, many of the established Caribbean community within North Kensington section of Harrow Road in Northwest London and the surrounding areas have found constant solace at DJ's Caribbean Takeaway.

Opened in the summer of 1992 by Mark and Viona Davidson as an outpost for Caribbean food, DJs, with its trademark green and yellow tiles paying homage to Jamaica. The takeout spot quickly grew to be a crowd pleaser on the long stretch of road between Regent's Park in central London and the outer points of northwest London such as Harlesden, Wembley and Harrow. This was more apparent as Caribbean communities had begun to be eschewed from inner areas of West London such as Notting Hill and Ladbroke Grove over years. In a time where the Caribbean takeout scene was scarce and more often than not was centred around bakeries, DJs looked to provide something different.

From the beginning, DJs went beyond the regular Caribbean food fixtures like curries and incorporated varieties of Asian-inspired dishes like Chow Mein noodles that for many years have been popular in the Caribbean due to the region's mixed heritage. All this helped in attracting commerce from the mosaic of other migrant communities that make up the local London area where DJs is located.

Given the success of the first shop, it was natural that yearning for DJs' food at events across the country would follow. The couple, alongside a growing team, spent years catering for private events as well as for charities, housing associations, and local council departments that built their profile to the stage that people demanded more. In response to this, in 2005 the couple took over an ailing pub nearby in Cricklewood and renamed it Heritage Inn Rhum Bar as a way of having an institution dedicated to preserving and celebrating Caribbean culture.

With a weekly timetable jammed with events such as Monday's Cuban salsa and Kizomba sessions and Tuesday's dominos night, all the way through to Sunday slow jams music night the Davidson's in everything they did strove to ensure that all elements of Caribbean culture stayed alive in the area. The Heritage Inn ceased in the late 2010's after the couple stepped back from the business but their imprint in the local landscape of Caribbean food is inescapable.

Buzzrocks

Hulme, Manchester

Few food establishments in Manchester have to deal with queues forming before opening their gates on a rainy weekday morning, but after more than two decades serving up his charismatic take on Caribbean food, scenes at Basil "Buzzrock" Anderson's "Buzzrocks" restaurant reflect just that. Also hailing from a heritage of culinary folklore in Manchester, the father of Basil's wife Farida Anderson was founder of the city's legendary Plaza Cafe (Charlie's) on Upper Brook Street that between the 1970s and 1990s bewildered revellers with their "Suicide" and "Killer" strength curries.

Coming to Manchester from Jamaica in 1976 as a young man, the origins of Buzzrocks were far more nomadic than the slick operation seen today. Hanging out with friends into the late hours of the night, Basil would offer up his cooking talents and recalls it was here where he got the nickname that has stuck with him to this day. "They used to say I would make my dumplings so tight. Tight like rocks!" proclaims Basil aka 'Buzzrock'.

Where Caribbean meals were prior often the reserve of late nights at clubs like the Nile or Reno and a few select outlets, a now confident Basil sought to create a legitimate outlet for his food. Charming crowds at events like the Moss Side Carnival, he bought a garden gazebo, had a welder friend whip him up a proper steel jerk drum and he was on his way. After about a year however, the gazebo wasn't adequate enough for all the demand.

Needing to upgrade, in the early 1990s Basil travelled down to Haverford West in the heart of neighbouring Wales to source one from the traveller community that he'd heard had a deft hand for furnishing quality and affordable trailers.

"We were like the Jamaican travellers," Farida chimes in. With success at the likes of Glastonbury and Womad festivals, Basil soon found fare touring around the country. "Every carnival! Every festival! We'd go to one, finish for the day, pack up and head straight to the next one" and with Basil needing to meticulously clean his jerk drum every day, Farida recalls they were often the first in and last out at every event.

The daily toll of moving a freezer van and dealing with muddy landscapes synonymous with outdoor English events eventually became a bit too much. He jestingly admits, "The trailer wasn't hygienic and it was never really big enough." In the colder climates, Basil recalls "It got so cold I couldn't even open the trailer sometimes. I had to light a fire with the gas just to open it!" Regardless, demand had long since overtaken supply in the 16ft trailer.

After a few years and some wrangling with the local council, the Hulme location was established in 2007 where he and team work their way around a pristine open kitchen.

Few realise that in order to prepare the shops numerous dishes featuring an assortment of secret gravies, sauces and spices by midday means that Basil has already been on his feet for at least six hours prior. Not divulging any hidden clues, Basil does suggest, "Absolutely nothing's frozen! Everything is fresh!"

Waking up no later than 5am, Basil travels to the city's Smithfield wholesale market to source ingredients for the day and to also send greetings to the venders he's gotten to know over the years. With food in tow, these are meticulously incorporated into many of the staple meals. Snacks like the jerk chicken wrap and Buzzrock's "Hot Flashes" wings doused in his concoction of spices and "chicken splits" (chicken cuts served inside the marquee Buzzrock fried dumplings) are convenient options for those on the go.

For those with a bit more time on their hands, Buzzrock's Jamaican lamb (unfortunately not still £3.50 like they were in his 1990s trailer,) remain as alluring as they were over twenty years ago. As a veteran Rasta, expect to find zero traces of pork in Buzzrocks. However, with rotisserie chicken, succulent goat and oxtail on offer alongside sea bass and saltfish immersed in natural herbs very few have cause to complain.

Farida proclaims however that the most popular choice is the "Half n Half," (pictured) a mixture of rice & peas and chips. This combination of Caribbean and Northern British staples is a prime example of the makeup of Buzzrock's dining area on any given day. Here, first timers to Caribbean food sit side by side with long-time residents of the area who reminisce on Buzzrock's mobile antics across every corner of the city.

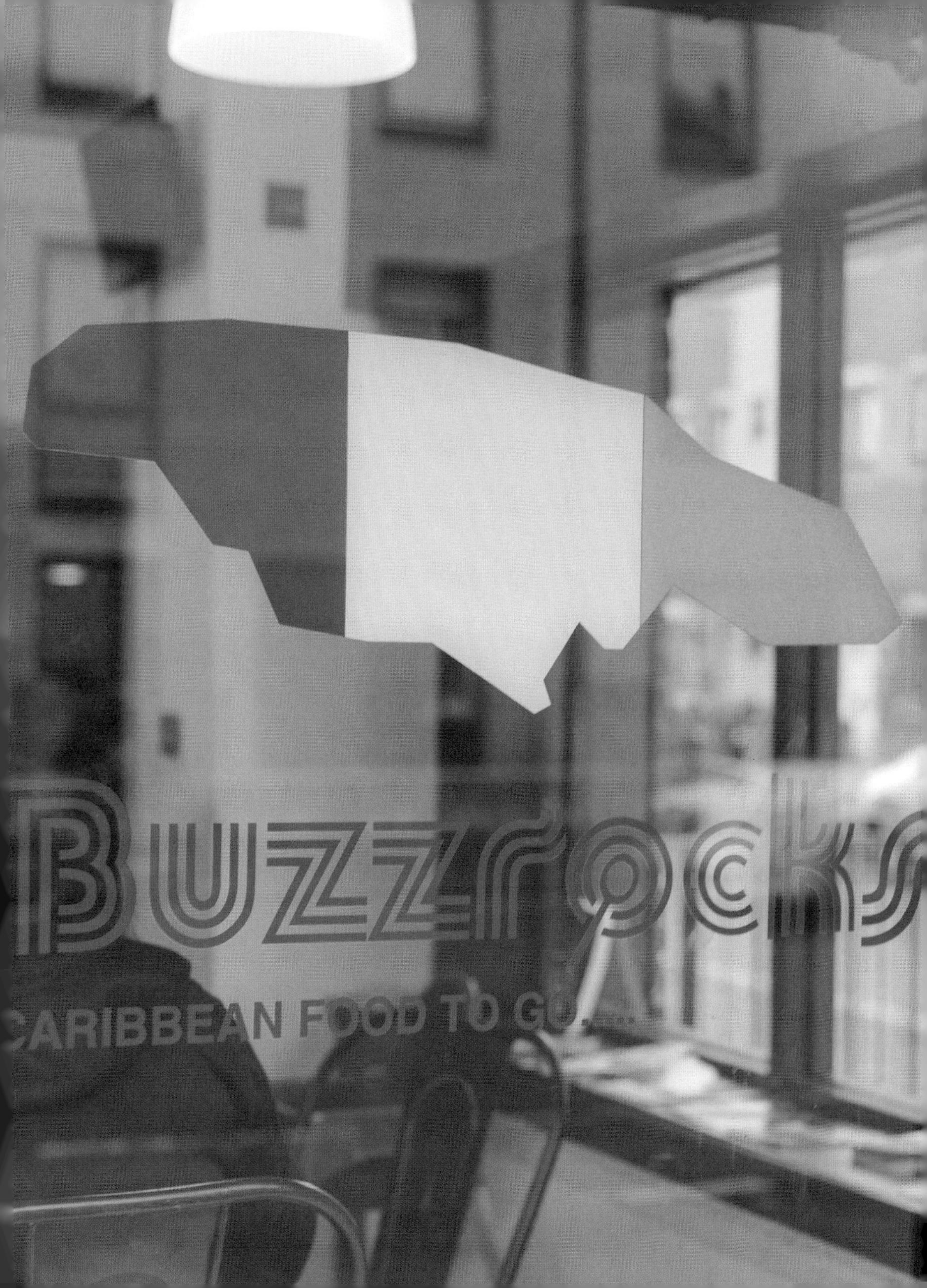
Buzzrocks
CARIBBEAN FOOD TO GO

Peppers & Spice
North London

In the mid 1990s a TV sketch show called The Real McCoy shown on the UK's BBC network had hit peak popularity. Satirising the everyday of Black and Asian life in the UK, one particular sketch that hit home for many was a ridicule of the experience of buying Caribbean food in Britain called "Misery's West Indian Restaurant." Many found humour for example in the terrible customer service and frequent unavailability of food, partially perhaps as it was based on some truths. In 1997, with a vision of changing this perception Mr. Berrick Griffiths alongside many family members founded one of London's favourites Peppers & Spice.

Coming to England from eastern Jamaica's Westmoreland Parish, Berrick's earliest memories of Caribbean food in his new homeland were in the animated setting of East London's Ridley Road Market, where newly situated families from Eastern Europe, the Caribbean and later on Turkey and Vietnam would all congregate to source crucial shopping list items that couldn't be found at the bigger supermarkets. Without these markets it probably wouldn't have been possible for Berrick to have his own favourite "Oxtail and rice & peas or Yellow yam, cornmeal dumpling and cow foot."

Having previously ventured into the commerce side of food through past Caribbean outing Take Two in the late 1980s and early 1990s, he was already well versed in the acumen needed to grow and expand a chain of restaurants. Consequently, when the opportunity for Peppers & Spice arose, already being very familiar with the Dalston area the family made a move. "There was a need for good Caribbean food," Berrick explains, somewhere with "Good value for money and consistency in the food." Presenting this in a transparent and family-orientated environment made all the difference to the scores of people in the area during the late 1990s and the people who came then and still come back today, but now with children and grandchildren.

The term "Peppers & Spice" acts as a representation of the foundations of Caribbean food including the frequent use of scotch bonnet peppers. Whilst the shop is unmistakably Jamaican in its roots, as seen by the green and yellow colourway with frequent homages its national bird, the Hummingbird, the shop has made an overwhelming attempt at encompassing various facets of all Caribbean walks of life in its grand daily changing menu.

With Tottenham branch head chef Tex leading a team cooking anything from breakfast porridges, to the cod-based coley fish, snapper fish, jerk chicken, myriad of soups and elaborately designed pasta dishes (pictured) all simultaneously from morning to sunset, the options are often endless. As Dez, Berrick's nephew laughingly tells, "Some people want a full dinner at 9am! Oxtail, rice n peas, curry goat – they want it all!"

With Peppers and Spice existing how it has for two decades as a family business, Caribbean food has been a way of life as countless relatives of Berrick have, and still continue to work, within the two stores in Dalston and Tottenham. This constant of cheerful faces (one of them being Berrick's sister, international Gospel singer-songwriter Sister Pansy who's posters feature around the Dalston shop) and signature flaky patties have played a sizeable role in Peppers & Spice becoming one of the most popular destinations for Caribbean food over the years as seen by the meandering out-of-the-door queues commonly seen at both stores.

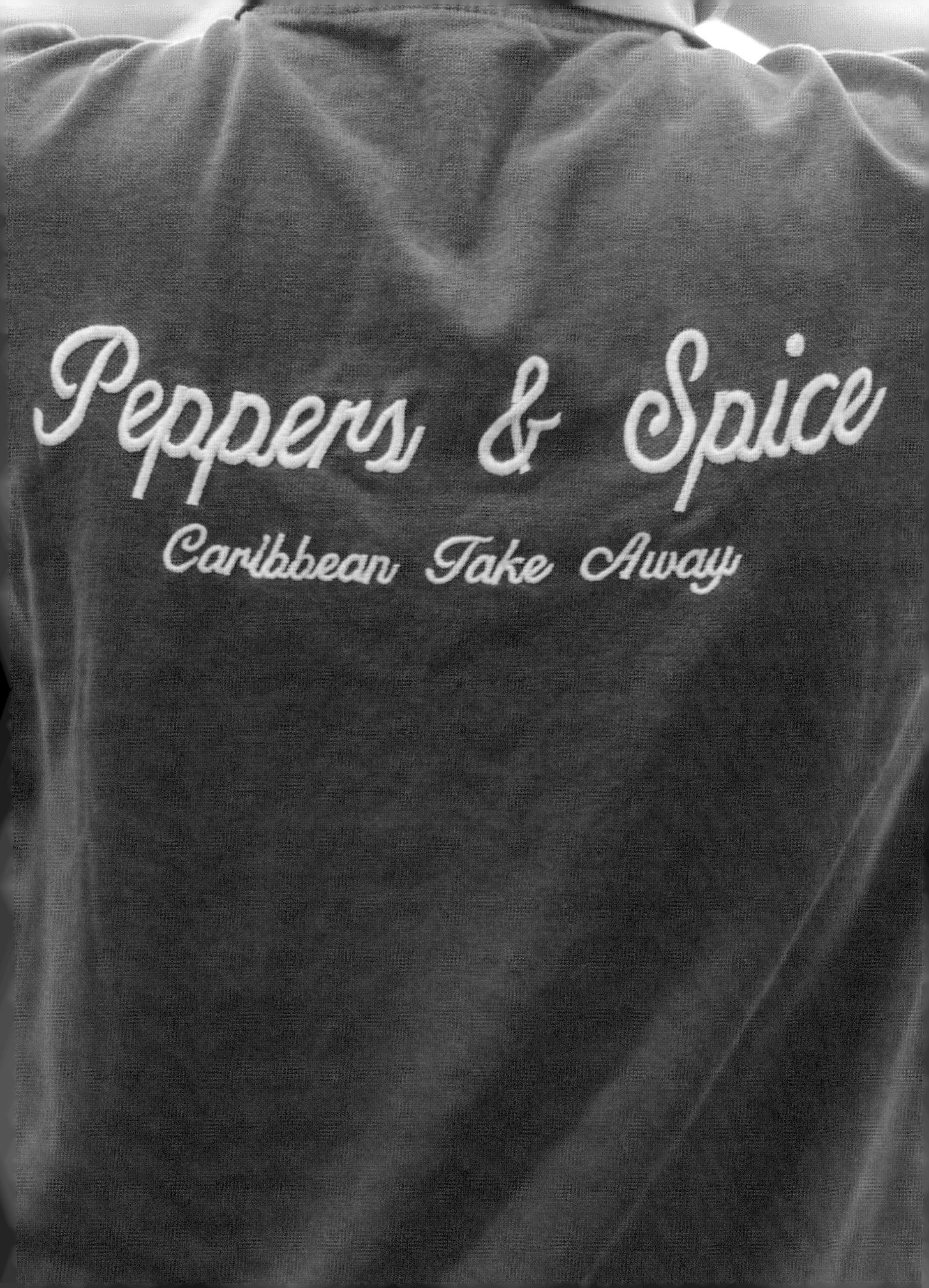
Peppers & Spice
Caribbean Take Away

Aunt Sally's
West Midlands

With its origins dating back to the early 1990s, Aunt Sally's - as tenderly grown over the years to become the largest Caribbean chain in the West Midlands and one the few multi-city Caribbean chains across the U.K.

With humble beginnings in a midlands city deprived of Caribbean eateries but a burgeoning Caribbean community, at age 50 "Aunty Sally" made a strikingly bold move in the face of oncoming retirement and opened the first store at 15 Worcester Street in Wolverhampton. Growing up in a mountainous village called Cold Spring in Eastern Westmoreland, Jamaica cooking the traditional meals of the island was a lifelong pastime and translating this love into a business after nearly two decades of living in the UK came naturally. Furthermore, with a continued tenure of providing charitable community sustenance, primarily in the city's Zion City Church a transition into commerce with an array of Caribbean delicacies was well received.

Having served the midlands community for much of the early to mid 1990s the family's initial venture came to a hault after the city centre began to transition elsewhere. However, the brand was able to sustain its name through years of functions and catering supplemented with Aunt Sally's son providing Caribbean ready meals for numerous city councils across the region. Through this, in 2007 with more experience behind them and a sustained name the family relaunched nearby on Broad Street and found rapid favour after they began staying open til the late

hours of the morning to cater to nearby students. Finding favour with this student base, the shop suggests this also helped grew a diverse audience for the food outside just the Caribbean community.

With a shop moniker that created a friendly face that represented the ethos of good customer service to defeat oftentimes-negative stereotypes of Caribbean customer service this is epitomized by Aunt Sally's grandson and company manager Daniel Simpson, who often can be found personally delivering meals himself across Birmingham. As he suggests "If the food is good the people will come," and off the back of Aunt Sally's veteran light, non-greasy dumplings, boneless mutton and home-made Apple Crumble and Caribbean Punch the repeat custom across the midlands is far from a surprise.

Consequently, expansion into nearby cities of Birmingham and Walsall seemed almost inevitable and through this, Aunt Sally was able to accomplish a long-term personal goal of providing stability for her family. As Aunt Sally herself gracefully put it "leaving a legacy for her sons, grandchildren and great grandchildren."

As Daniel eludes "It was important to keep the culture alive but we thought there was a gap in places that appeal to a new generation." With many of the younger family members at the helm, Aunt Sally's has placed an emphasis on representing a younger culture from the diaspora and bringing the culture of a Caribbean experience into the modern day. Their famed slow cooked Oxtail, seasoned chicken options and hot pepper prawns no doubt aide this shift too.

Maureen's

Roundhay, Leeds

Things had all gotten a bit too much for Maureen by the time the entirety of Chapeltown were queuing out her front door and down the road for a rare taste of Caribbean cuisine, which at the time was not widely available in 1980s Leeds.

Maureen who was born and raised in the area around Chapeltown Road in northern Leeds carried on a practice not too unfamiliar in places across the Caribbean like St. Kitts where Maureen's family originated. This was a form of open door policy where local familiar faces might pop into a neighbour's house for dinner and a chat in the hours after a long day.

Having a long-standing passion for cooking, Maureen found great pleasure in sharing her wares with the local community who had limited options at the time for Caribbean food. Being the close-knit community that it was (the legacy of which remains today) word spread like wildfire to the neighbouring areas of Leeds and soon after Maureen had the walk-in numbers of a restaurant at her humble abode. "I would start cooking at midday – fried chicken, jerk chicken, with cakes or crumble with custard for afters, and when the food was done it was done!" Maureen recollects. "I always had random people coming through and the queues just kept getting bigger and bigger. It really became too much when I had my kids running around all the people." Thankfully, they picked up some good skills as Maureen proudly attests that they can all cook very well.

"I'd always wanted a shop of my own to cook in," Maureen reveals, and in 2003 this turned into a reality when a premises became available in Chapeltown's bordering area of Roundhay. Maureen saw the opening of her shop not as a brand new venture but rather an extension of the previous enterprise in her kitchen. "I wanted to keep the same open kitchen vibe here so people could see what I'm giving them – In some places you place an order and then they go into the back and come back with your meal all wrapped up." Comparing to how people back in the days at her house would always pick out their preferred piece of meat, Maureen adds, "Here you can see how they chop, prepare and simmer food" and she believes it adds a level of authenticity to the food.

After word spread that city hero Rio Ferdinand, a star footballer who once played for the nearby Leeds United, was a fan, a local newspaper got hold of the news and proclaimed Maureen to be "A new woman in Rio's Life!" This news however may have been to the displeasure of the thousands of other Maureen fans who feared they might have lost her cooking talents to the football ace. "I just love cooking," Maureen asserts and not just content with cooking in one spot over the years she made sure to become a key fixture at many of the city's reggae and dancehall concerts every year as well as Leeds' vivid and colourful West Indian Carnival.

As a collection of regulars stream in the shop throughout the day, those fortunate enough to gain a dine-in spot on the glossed wooden tables await patiently as the chefs pour in and out of the open kitchen serving up Maureen's unique take on Caribbean food. The fish dishes, including brown stew fish, fried and boneless fish dishes, which can be served with chips have proved a popular substitute for the British staple of battered Fish and Chips. As the day draws on Maureen's "Supreme Meals" also start to take precedent. The choice of two fish or two meat selections with a choice of classic sides proves too tempting a choice to pass up for most.

Given this, when pressed as to what she would serve if she could only serve just one dish, Maureen reveals, "It would have to be Oxtail!" mainly as a result of its naturally soft and sweet meat. Such a simplistic notion is quite the opposite of Maureen's plans however as she looks forward to expanding the space so she can make the kitchen a bit bigger.

Blessed Caribbean Takeaway

Loughborough Junction, SW London

Decorated with numerous images of magnificent Lions, Jamaican iconography and tricolored ornaments, Blessed West Indian Takeaway located between southeastern London's Camberwell and the more westerly Brixton is a place where people for some years have flocked for their regular dose of Caribbean food 24 hours a day. More often than not however, a fair few simply stop by to deliver a speedy "Wah Gwan!" to a particularly dapper gentleman behind the counter known as King Atarney (Or King I Tarney depending on the preference).

"Ha! That's just what they called me," recalls Atarney, more formally known as Tony Bailey. "That's the name people gave me back home," remembering a foregone time growing up in Kingston, Jamaica. Looking closely around the shop above the counter, amongst the grand Rastafarian depictions, are images of a young man immaculately fitted out in razor sharp suits and dazzling waistcoats. "A mi dat!" Atarney proclaims, still making sure to be as equally vigorous and colourfully dressed everyday without fail as he did back then. With food a later venture in life, Atarney details a long-standing and current passion for music.

Moving to England in 1986, Atarney advanced his everlasting love of music from back home as a music artist predominantly in the form of a vocalist. With this soulful brand of Reggae music, Atarney tells, "I used to record all over South London. I worked with so many people over the years! I performed at the Brixton Academy, Brockwell Park…so many places!"

Recording an album entitled "When it go end" with two stand out tracks being "Save Jamaica" a heart-warming prayer for his home nation and "Cowboy Traffic Warden." Illustrating Atarney's affable nature, a promo for the latter hanging in the shop announces a "hilariously funny new single championing the cause of drivers everywhere. Promising to make you laugh until your belly hurts." Quite simply "Ever had your car clamped – Are you vexed at the amount of parking tickets you have to pay? Are you a traffic warden? Then this tune is for you. CHECK IT!!!"

In similar fashion to a certain generation growing up in Jamaica, Atarney expresses how preparing food was just a part of life. "Back then I used to do jerk on a big grill in the area. I would cook for the whole community." Hence, when the opportunity to become the full principal at Blessed emerged in the 1990s, Atarney became fully involved. Recreating a furnace of a jerk grill in the kitchen, familiar in stature to anyone who has been fortunate to witness an authentic beachfront jerk hut, Atarney has carried on this tradition.

Always wanting to create a varied menu, Atarney reminisces on his early days in London during the 1980s, "You could get some of the food in the grocery shops but there wasn't too many places where it was cooked." With the colossal menu at hand, for newcomers Atarney reveals, "For new people I always tell them get either jerk chicken, goat or oxtail. They will always like one of those three." This tactic ensures return custom so Atarney can entice them further down the well of his menu. Stewed cow foot and stewed fish (pictured) both guest-star alongside Blessed's chicken sandwiches (jerk, grilled or fried) housed in coco bread that undoubtedly overshadows offerings from the nearby chicken and chips shops.

With food running in the family, any and every meal (apart from the long list of cakes and deserts) should be accompanied by Atarney's son's all-purpose jerk seasoning sauce also known as "Lightning Blessed!" The title alone lets would-be triers know what they are in for.

Ochi

Shepard's Bush, W London

The webpage of Ochi's Caribbean Takeaway describes loud and proud that it was opened on 17th August 1996 in order to pay homage to the birth date of one of Jamaica's foremost national heroes Marcus Garvey – an internationally renowned political activist and intellectual.

Marcus Garvey, alongside another Jamaican national treasure Bob Marley, were both born in the northern most parish of Jamaica, St Ann's, containing the epicentre of the famed Dunn's River waterfall and the town of Ocho Rios where the Ochi restaurant name is derived from. The derivation of the name Ocho Rios is debated though the name translates as "Eight Rivers" in Spanish. Some believe the name to be a native take of the Spanish term Las Chorreras meaning "waterfall" or "sprout" - both a relic of past Spanish imperialism on the island.

Ironically, St. Ann's Parish, as the point of many firsts in Jamaica, the first landing spot of Africans to Jamaica, the first Spanish capital of Jamaica and opening visual to the first James Bond film Dr. No - Ochi restaurant through the years has become many of West London's residents and transients' first contact to the culinary element of Jamaican culture.

Since it was opened by Janet Long and family in the mid 1990s Ochi's location on Uxbridge road with its close proximity to the internationally acclaimed venues of Shepard's Bush Empire and Hammersmith Apollo has lead Ochi to become the go-to venue for countless world famous artists, especially those from the Caribbean needing a taste of back home on their forays further into Europe.

From floor to ceiling, Ochi's wall of fame exists as a testament to this service with signed posters of musicians, actors and entertainers to rival any restaurant in London, let alone a Caribbean restaurant. The ever-affable Dom, who has been managing the shop with his mother, exclaims that there are dozens more they just haven't had time or space to display.

One of the many signed posters from Barbados' darling and superstar singer Rihanna that reads "To all my friends and fans at Ochi – Best Jamaican Food!" sits aside a glowing menu board of peppered steak, stew peas, curry goat, oxtail and jerk chicken. This only comprises but a fraction of Ochi's offering. Dom's jovial nature and frequent jokes with the drivers and chefs helps keep a high spirit in the kitchen, who as Dom explains, cook throughout the entire day rather than just cooking a few batches of the days meal and leaving them to rest. This has kept a common flow of zealous mouths to feed whether it is a commute in from further west regions such as Acton and Ealing into Central London or vice versa at the end of the day.

Etana

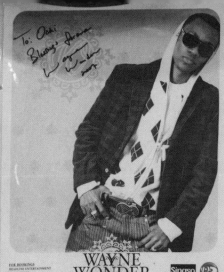

WAYNE
WONDER

Singso

TUFF GONG
INTERNATIONAL

DAMIAN
JR. GONG
MARLEY

RCH 11TH

FIZZ&BOOG

John Holt
1947-2014

CAPLETON

FREDDIE

MCGREGOR

ELEPHANTMAN

the debut album

COMIN' 4 YOU !

LEMAR

Leroy Gibbon

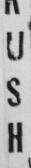

KUSHI

NUFF

MEAT MEALS

Brown Stew Chicken	£ 6.00	£ 8.00
Curry Chicken	£ 6.00	£ 8.00
Jerk Chicken	£ 6.00	£ 8.00
Oxtail	£ 6.00	£ 8.00
Curry Goat	£ 6.00	£ 8.00
Stew Peas *(Wed Sat)*	£ 6.00	£ 850
Pepper Steak	£ 6.00	£ 8.00

To Ohci
Junior R
Mr. Love Jones

JUNIOR KELLY

VicRac
ENTERTAINMENT INC

For Management &
Bookings:
Ph: 212.629.0078 /
917.642.1543
E-mail: vicrac@hotmail.com

To Ochi

I-OCTANE

Bookings Contact :
Arrows Recording Company Ltd.
Tel: 876-928-2941 Cell: 876-352-3859
New Image Promotions 876-302-6590
Web Site: www.myspace.com/ioctanemusic
www.myspace.com/arrowsrecording www.arrowsrecording.com
Email: arrows@cwjamaica.com

YMES
NE BUT THE
CK ON FORM

USIC
ECIAL

MIS-TEEQ

Fake Love!
To Ochi!
Big up!
Sweet!
Love always
Alisha

TELSTAR

STA RHYMES
N WITH HIP HOP

Ochi
Respect
Bus A Bus

To Sweet
To Ochi
Crew
Bless

One Love
always

Cool Breeze

Hither Green, SE London

With the shop's double doors fully drawn on a warm summer's day, the name Cool Breeze seems highly apt. Opened in 1997 by Alice Muchanyuka and family, the name Cool Breeze reflects the calm, chilled out atmosphere in the shop and also hearkens back the serene mountains and meandering rivers from the likes of Danvers Pen and other locales dotted around the family's origins in Jamaica's St. Thomas.

After two decades in business, when asked the key to her success over the years, Alice replies, "Well there are many things, but most of what I know I learned from my older brother, Parker!" Whilst Alice recalls a time back in the mid 1990s when many people had not heard of Caribbean Food, Mr. Parker's recollections predate this by some time. "I came to England in 1960," Parker recalls. "I worked in the factories and such for a while but I wanted to do something else. In the late 1970s I had a place called Blue Moon in Bradford (Yorkshire) and then after that one called Starlight Restaurant on Manningham Lane. People just called it Parkers though!" Parker adds, searching his minds archive. "That was a real first time for people, none of the people up there had ever seen or heard of this food before. It was very different times, you couldn't get all our ingredients so we had to make do."

"We had to entice him down to London," Alice remarks of her older brother, who is now a frequent resident chef at Cool Breeze. Give or take a few years after this Alice wanted to go out on a limb and start her own business. Having been always based in southeast London, she and family knew the area well. "We sent out feelers in the area and eventually this place came up," Alice describes. "I remember it very clear. I'll never forget! On the first day I was so busy cooking and preparing that I forgot to get takeaway plates. I had to serve people on proper plates. People still come in and talk about that day."

Alice depicts moments of worry in the shop's early days. "That first day I took £16.20, and on the second day not much more. Then one day it jumped to £300, and then around £500 – I remember jumping for joy! Everyone who came in carried on coming in. Now we have babies from back then who have grown up with the shop and now they are regulars." That generational grounding also runs in Alice's own family with her proudly proclaiming, "Everyone cooks! I have nieces and nephews who can cook for everyone."

Taking heed of the vastly changing populace in the area, a long-standing thread that has always underpinned Alice's philosophy in the shop is that of variety. Alice forwards, "We don't just have daily soups but daily vegetable soups too," whilst Mondays and Thursdays provide a vegetarian take on a house favourite Ital red pea soup. "Caribbean food has so many elements from all over the world and that's how we can attract people from all over to try our food." With this, from the brown stew slow-cooked in the house's special sauce, callaloo & saltfish and the steamed fish, everyone has their own favourite dish however the mackerel rundown, which features a fusion of coconut milk and a blend of mixed spices provides a particularly worldly outburst of flavours in the mouth.

On a very special day a visit to Cool Breeze might see you in the background of Alice's niece Danielle shooting the web's next best media hit after having already filmed the award winning series "Dear Jesus" there. Although Alice is not in the kitchen herself as much these days, with a head chef also from St. Thomas filling the role, Alice ensures the menu always has something new for people to get stuck into adding, "I take pride in always making sure we have everything we say we have."

Kool Runnings
Manchester

Be it the student filled area of Fallowfield, The high street of Longsight or the more residential Chorlton Road in Hulme, for the people of Manchester craving a spot of Caribbean food, for over twenty years Kool Runnings has guaranteed that all corners of the city's appetites could in some way be satisfied.

The restaurant's name, which immediately makes many recall the famous 1990s film of the same name featuring the iconic Jamaican bobsleigh team, has long been a catch phrase across the English speaking Caribbean islands meaning "Peace be the journey," or literally "Safe Journey." Just as well, since most of those who over the years have ventured to Kool Runnings rarely fail to return.

With the radius of Kool Runnings' operation falling within near proximity of English football goliaths Manchester United's Old Trafford Stadium and Manchester City's legendary Maine Road, the fierce passion with which long timers defend and support Kool Runnings could match either of those fan bases.

For this take on a highly a acclaimed jerk chicken and pimento allspice laden curry goat, frequent returners have a Mr. Aval Saunders to be grateful for. Born in Jamaica, Aval came over to Manchester as a teenager for a short vacation and had he returned as originally intended, today's Kool Running's may never have existed. Having met people in Jamaica who had already lived and experienced the British Isles before coming over he settled into life in England's Northern climate with a perceived relative ease.

Growing up in an agricultural environment, with his father finding employment as a farmer across various plantation fields reaping and sowing crops like peas, corn, tomatoes, cucumbers and so on whilst managing herds of lively cows and goats, it appears that some continuation of this practice would ensue at some point in the future. Traversing his way through a different career path in his early years, when the opportunity to become a chef at a local Caribbean restaurant presented itself he obliged. This eventually provided the genesis for Kool Runnings.

The shops in Manchester found good standing with locals with an abundance of indulgences like the jerk burgers, tangy sweet & sour prawns, callaloo stuffed bake fish and a hearty steak stew. However, for long time patrons, the mobile van situated next to the Sharon Pentecostal Church on Hulme's Chorlton Road on route to Whalley Range holds the most nostalgia for the humble beginnings of Kool Runnings.

Here, throughout the early part of the day queues form in a rapid fashion akin to flash mobs and soon after, before the late afternoon, once bursting platters of minted diced lamb, steamed fish, curried steak with accompanying vegetable rice and steamed vegetables have vanished.

149

Roti Joupa

London

Sometimes mistaken as an Asian curry house, the constant energetic Soca music emanating from the shop's speakers confirm that the family behind Roti Joupa hail from Trinidad & Tobago. Originally based on Southwest London's Clapham High Street, opened in the early 2000s the shop has gone from strength to strength opening shops in North and West London. Each of these shops is likely the only option close by for people craving a taste of the eastern Caribbean shores. More so, unfortunately this desire usually can't be satisfied to the fullest by the scores of Jamaican-owned restaurants in the capital.

With the British colonial legacy of transplanting many of those from South-eastern Asia to the Caribbean as indentured labourers, the similarities in the food are apparent with the cuisine and knowhow that naturally followed over the years. As the population of these people from the Indian subcontinent were larger to the east of the Caribbean than they were in the west, their foods and customs became more prevalent and customary.

While the similarities with staple Caribbean dishes such as curry goat, chicken or lamb and rice & peas can be seen, the meat free, Southeast Asian influences seep through with familiar sounding sides like bhaji (of the spinach kind), garlic bodi (string beans), channa aloo (chick peas), and curried aloo (potato). Traditionally to Trinidad and Tobago, much emphasis is placed on the vibrant pilau (or pelau) rice amongst its other rice selections.

While South London over the years has become a focal point for Caribbean food, not just for Londoners but people from all over Britain, few catered to the growing Trini community that had swelled within the Caribbean populace. This community was originally served by shops such as Quashie's and Trinbago dotted across London that have now unfortunately since departed. The Singh family, led by Robin, Savi and others stepped in to fill this void.

Donning Trinidadian red-and-white aprons, the crew can often be seen well into the late hours of the night topping up their assortment of tilapia (a highly seasoned fried fish,) and other rarities such as curried shrimp and duck. These can stand alone as main dishes but evidently most prefer them neatly wrapped up into the shop's specialty – roti. As the restaurant information describes "with its roots in India, the humble roti crossed the ocean to the Caribbean in the mid 1800s through many generations." With this, it's clear Roti Joupa aims to honour this heritage for another era.

With its open counter it is possible to peek into every nook and cranny of the shop. With this, Roti Joupa (Joupa being a creole interpretation of the word 'Hut') is a first-hand education in roti making from start to finish. The base of the preeminent style of roti – dhal puri, made at Joupa stuffed with ground lentils, jeera (cumin) and fresh seasonings emerges from the rear of the shop before being adequately shaped and then laid to rest on a trini-style oven top tawa (metal place) to cook. A special folding technique is employed for the secondary buss-up shot roti that results in a form of broken flatbread so soft many simply buy it as a snack to eat alone.

While many Jamaican-based establishments have sought to incorporate roti into their menus over the last few years, what sets Roti Joupa apart is the array of vibrant sides made free of artificial colours and flavourings. These extras are found rarely elsewhere in London let alone the UK. Crowd favourite "Hot" Doubles, a sandwich consisting of two turmeric-based baras (flatbread deep fried in an iron clad Dutch pot – pictured next page) filled with curry chickpeas and sweet tamarind sauce, are a runaway example of this.

For those with a definitive sweet tooth, Joupa utilises its baking practices to create snacks almost irresistible to avoid once eaten. Trini fudge, kurma, (similar to a Mexican churro,) doughy snacks glazed in cinnamon with sugar and the sticky tamarind fruit balls all under £1.50 give anyone willing to try the impetus. Decorated in tropical decals, beachfront paintwork and art of Trinidad's national flower, the chaconia, the affable spirit of the whole staff always ensures a fun outing at Roti Joupa.

TRY OUR FRESH HOMEMADE ROTI (THIN, FLAT, ROUNDED PANCAKE LIKE BREAD) COOKED ON A TRADITONAL TAWA (METAL PLATE). WITH IT'S ROOTS IN INDIA, THE HUMBLE ROTI CROSSED THE OCEAN TO THE CARIBBEAN IN THE MID 1800s. THROUGH MANY GENERATIONS, THE ROTI IS A TRADITIONAL DISH EATEN WITH MOST MEALS.

ROTI

PLAIN
DHAL PURI	1.50
BUSS-UP SHOT	1.25

WITH MEAT
CURRY CHICKEN	5.50
STEW CHICKEN	5.50
CURRY LAMB	5.50
CURRY GOAT	5.50
CURRY SHRIMP	5.50
CURRY DUCK	5.50
FRIED FISH (TILAPIA)	5.50

WITH VEGETABLE
CURRY ALOO (POTATO)	3.00
CHANNA (CHICK PEAS)	3.50
GARLIC BODI (STRINGBEANS)	4.00
PUMPKIN	4.00
BHAJI (SPINACH)	4.00
MIXED VEG (ALL OF THE ABOVE)	4.50

PARATHA (BUSS UP SHOT)
ROTI MADE WITH A SPECIAL FOLDING TECHNIQUE, RESULTING IN A SOFT, LIGHT & TASTY BREAD

MEAT ROTI
DHAL PURI WITH CHICKEN CURRY

DHAL PURI
ROTI FILLED WITH GROUND LENTILS, JEERA (CUMIN) AND FRESH SEASONINGS

IMAGES SHOWN ARE FOR GUIDANCE ONLY

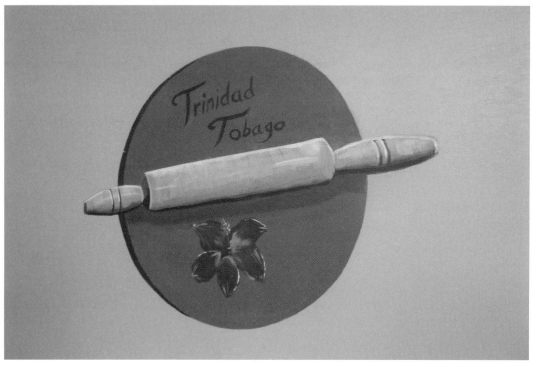

George's

First Jerk Catering

Surrey Street Market, Croydon

Where classical music composer Samuel Coleridge-Taylor may have once been seen walking the streets, Surrey Street Market has become a gathering place for many within the Croydon area. Records of a street market in Croydon related to the sale of food and general wares date back over 800 years. It was only in 1922 when the street market was taken over by the corporation of Croydon that the market was officially expanded Monday through Saturday and the impetus for the market as its experienced today was born.

At the southern point of the market opposite a vibrant flower seller, from 10am, George Whatle, proprietor of First Jerk hustles fervently under a blue and yellow tarpaulin serving many of the daily market ramblers. Although the outpost has an official name, many who frequent simply refer to it as "George's" or "Jerk George." Over 15 years in the market, since the early 2000s, George enjoyed being a first mover of sorts to the market regarding hot "and good tasting" food, as it was primarily just fruit and vegetables traders before he took up stock at the market. In the early days George explains how he personally went around with flyers promoting his new business to the offices and local tradespeople around the Croydon area.

This level of initiative was nothing new to George, as a young salesman across the plains of Jamaica, he describes how selling garments at iconic Jamaican markets such as Linsted Market in St. Catherine's, St. Ann's Brownstown Market and Clarendon's May Pen Market made him more than ready for trade in Britain.

After coming to London in 1993, years of cutting hair for some North London's finest helped him to grow his profile. "I used to cut Ian Wrights hair," although he teasingly proclaims he has since hung up his Arsenal FC shirt due to their lacklustre form in recent years.

Standing with George any later than 1.30pm, any conversation is customarily interrupted by a stream of apologies from George. This is not regarding bad service but rather the number of customers perturbed by the fact George is routinely sold out by this time and their tardiness means another day without his home prepped food. As he exclaims "whether its rainy or sunny – the food done same way!" although rain can often dampen the mood of the day, George explains he thought about moving from the market to a physical premises but the traditional hassle of a brick and mortar enterprise wasn't worth it. Plus as he suggests, "You meet so many nice people here in the market," given the transient nature of the market contributes to the wide variety of people who pass through on a daily basis.

Cooking since the age of 7, he has developed an almost psychic ability to predict the food mood of the day. Switching from rice 'n peas some days to pumpkin rice, he prefers to mix it up every day. Giving some insight to his virtuosity, "You can come every day and get something completely different," leaving some element of surprise for customers. This he believes has contributed much to his 15 year plus tenure. "You have to know when to cook a small goat and when to cook a cow," all of which are sourced from the local market butchers who usually come for a taste at the end of a day's shift.

George's very presence in the market is a testimony to his passion for food. Enduring two brain surgeries after a stroke in 2010, George returned to the market just two years later and while he has fleeting vision in one eye, he jokingly declares that it doesn't matter "I could cook blind!" The only shame is most days "When the Food done – it Done!" and he doesn't even get to eat his own food, savouring every last piece of flavour for his customers, who start texting for requests before he's even out of bed.

Iree Island

Walthamstow, E London

In the midst of a sun-stroked day, when Iree Island's double doors are fully drawn and the table and chairs sprawl out onto the adjoining Walthamstow Market, the restaurant lives up to its name as eastenders from all walks of life stream in for meals throughout the course of a day.

The hybrid of fresh salads and pasta assortments added to the emblematic Caribbean dishes have proved a hit in the area and as most finish up their meals like the ever popular soup offerings (pictured) leaving bone-dry plates they usually bid a ecstatic farewell to the staff and owner-head chef Anthony Brown, known widely as Flash, if he's to be found in the kitchen at that time.

Never originally intending to enter the food world, Flash (whose tag came from the coincidence of sharing a name with infamous Jamaican Hot Stepper Anthony Brown, and hence locals would call him by the name of Brown's notorious partner George Flash,) quickly climbed up the chef ranks as a young teen in his hometown Negril, Jamaica. Operating in the kitchens of various upmarket hotel restaurants and resorts as a 14 year old, and becoming a head chef at the ripe age of 17, Flash developed his cooking techniques and palate. Here he would cook for various global music stars and international politicians.

As a serial entrepreneur in the UK, 'Flash' got his jumpstart in the industry during the mid 1990s working across the Caribbean food scene in London and supplying self-made patties to various establishments, including former hot spot Calypso, which now houses the location for Iree Island.

Flash describes himself as "East London through and through" since arriving in England some years ago from Jamaica. This is something that is represented in Flash's ideologies of self-sustainability in his business and creating an internal ecosystem to aide this. As well as sourcing food from East London, "We have a warehouse complex not too far from here, also in East London where we produce everything we sell here," Flash describes. With its British-made 6ft mixer, "The factory can produce a max capacity of 2000 patties that are baked and transported back to the shop throughout the day." The warehouse's patties have also become a popular snack for the residents and workers of the neighbouring churches and industry houses in the Leyton complex.

The space also is home to the production of many of Flash's takes on popular island drinks such as the highly regarded Guinness punch (pictured), whilst also providing a space for experimenting on after-jerk seasonings such as his pioneering rum and coffee sauce flavours, sweet snacks like the biscuit gizzada treats and the crunchy peanut and coconut drops. While some of the side dishes such as the well-liked Caribbean style mac n cheese, fritters and such can be prepped at the restaurants kitchen, the space affords a level of upscaling that Flash alludes has helped the business greatly.

Flash remarks, "The best idea is to have an idea that is a good idea!" As a frequent traveller of the world, with an emphasis on Africa, delving into a world of different tastes, Flash may have some more eccentric food-based aces up his sleeve in the near future.

Bluejay Café
South Norwood, S. London

Walking down Portland Road, in the outer reaches of South London at times can almost feel like a stroll around the namesake Portland parish of Jamaica. With Caribbean takeaways, grocery shops, barbers and more lining the long road, the area is one of the few that could vie for the title of London's little Jamaica. At the centre of this hub is Dave and Joy Blake's Bluejay Café.

The roots of the café go back to the Blake's early childhoods. Jamaican born Joy who grew up living with her grandmother was introduced to cooking at a very early age. This travelled with her as she made the transatlantic voyage to south London whilst still a young child. On arrival Joy details, "being the eldest child I was taken into the kitchen by my mother and my father and shown how to cook the family meal." She adds, "cooking for my mum, dad and siblings and that's where my passion came from." Not long later Joy describes how she would begin to experiment with cookbooks and recipes one day even cooking beef stroganoff instead of the usual Caribbean curries and this sparked her wider cooking interest.

Joy details her various career paths that eventually led to the food industry. "One day my cousin asked me to come in his shop on a Saturday at his bakery and Caribbean takeaway shop." Through working at her cousin's shop, she met Dave, her future husband. Dave was a seasoned baker and he had also trained up as a chef at Rules Restaurant, one of the oldest culinary institutions central London. Joy continues, "one day we decided together that we would open our own business" and they decided to start looking for opportunities in the south London vicinity. When the bid on the shop was accepted the couple immediately started to plan. With this blank canvas of commercial space, Joy explains, "we knew what we wanted to do. A nice café environment and a patio." The entire family even got together and planned the whole menu as Joy ensured, "we wanted to make sure our menu was different."

Through customer feedback and rigorous trial and error over the years, they found a happy medium between Caribbean end English flavours. The 'build your own breakfast' is the best demonstration of this with endless combinations featuring the likes of ackee and saltfish, mackerel, yam and green banana as well as baked beans, hash browns, eggs, sausages and much more. "Everyone loves the Caribbean and the different options that we have." So much so that

people venture to the café deep into the evening for their breakfast. The rest of the menu is a smash hits compilation of Caribbean dining. There are a multitude of fish dishes, curries and stews and a growing cohort of meals to satiate the growing number of vegetarians and vegans in the area.

The space opened in 2008 and while you get the feeling it has been around for decades longer things weren't always plain sailing. Joy gives off the aura that her determined positive mindset begets aided by 6am starts, meditation and healing crystals that line the shop. Things were quiet in the early days and she even recalls being happy that they totalled £26 one day. "We stuck at it, we kept updating the website, pushing word of mouth, flyering…" This perseverance led to legendary status the café has today.

Five minutes spent inside this café, be it dining in or awaiting takeaway and you can feel the communal importance. While many restaurants seek to highlight the myriad of celebrity clientele (and many are known to frequent this place,) here the opposite happens, instead celebrating the regulars covering the walls with photo snapshots of hundreds of local customers, friends and family.

Joy emotionally recounts, "people are bumping into each they haven't seen for years" adding, "it's a mothers meeting place with babies, we have large celebrations people use Bluejay for." People of all ages and walks of life often come to Blue Jay's and the couple for assistance on counselling, like skills and more. Joy illuminates, "in my role I feel I'm wearing many different hats. Sometimes I'm more than the person behind that counter…I'm mum, aunty, sister a lot of things to the customers." With all this, "Blue Jay provides a space where our customers can come and feel comfortable.

Roti Stop

Stoke Newington, N London

"The parties were crazy back then! Sometimes it was Friday, Saturday and Sunday – Sometimes it was two in one night," recalls Bernard Jackson otherwise justly known as "Roti King," owner and chef at north London's Roti Stop. A selection of photos in the front of Bernard's Stoke Newington shop recalls the early days before the shop when Roti Stop operated from a nomadic van enrapturing many people with its Caribbean, but specifically Trinidadian, specialty of food.

"I used to drive around London selling the food myself," Bernard elucidates. Starting in 1991, travelling to as many carnivals as possible, Bernard tells around this time, "I used to target the Trini (Trinidadian) parties across London, we called them Fête's. One of the main clubs was Dougies," first opened in 1983 by Mr. Irvine Douglas who had previously owned a popular North London club restaurant called Dougies' Hideaway that was established back in 1976.

"I used to drive and set up as the parties were winding down and the people were leaving the club," says Bernard, "It used to be jokes, there was no order – the queues were mad...The party scene used to be crazy, All the top Soca DJs and artists came over. The vibe was hot! Many people still remember me from those days."

Endeavouring to keep as much of the original methodology of street-style cooking derived from his Trinidadian hometown of San Fernando in the urban setting of London, Bernard's hectic times on the road provided stepping stones into the culinary world before popularity outstripped his trusty steed of a van.

Since opening the Stoke Newington shop in 2007, Bernard's care and attention paid to each roti has confirmed his alias as Roti King. All roti ordered are instantly put to warm on what is known as a Tawah, or Tawa or Platin or Baking Stone, it depends on what part of the Caribbean you are from! - a cast iron pan placed on top of a hob. These Tawah's ensure the roti are heated through and through without compromising any of the original soft and flaky texture or adding any extra unwanted moistness.

Monday through Sunday, Bernard's wealth of roti offerings tempts in locals multiple times a week. Boneless curried lamb and chicken, or even jerk chicken provide an appetising gateway for newcomers not well versed in the art of handling bones found in the curry goat and stew chicken roti. Bernard also places equal focus on the non-meat eaters with his tried and tested fish and vegetable options. Whilst some other places may other think it crazy to order ackee and saltfish or fried fish in a roti, Bernard summons his Roti King wisdom to make it work impeccably.

All snacks including the chickpea sandwich and flatbread "Doubles" and split pea "Phulouri" balls should all be dabbed with some of Bernard's homemade "Highgrade" Caribbean hot sauce and washed down with his own batch of fresh juices. As a firm advocate of a healthy lifestyle, Bernard's homemade peanut and Guinness punches sit side by side a rich magenta coloured vegan punch based on soya milk blended with ginger, carrot and beetroot. For the more exploratory, mauby, a drink made from the bark of the mauby plant and sorrel, a flowering plant grown both found wildly across the Caribbean when pulsated with sugar and spices make refreshing options.

Lining the shop above the counter on the interior rustic wooden frames are currencies given to Bernard from customers descending from every corner of the Earth who have visited Roti Stop over the years. Relishing these opportunities to display his culture to a wide audience the shop is equally stock with books of Caribbean culture and posters of how to cook traditional Trinidadian food for visitors to peruse should they unfortunately not be able to make it to the shop.

Bernard's Pholourie Balls, Roti, Vegan Juices and Plantain Skewers

36b

ROTI  STOP

Caribbean Takeaway

FULL RANGE OF CARIBBEAN FOOD TO TAKE AWAY

36b 36b

ROTI-STOP
Caribbean Cuisine
EAT-IN
or
TAKEAWAY

Smokey Jerkey

New Cross, SE London

"My home is the birthplace of Jerk!" announces a boisterous voice concealed by a plume of smoke shrouding the rear kitchen. This is a voice all too familiar with the Londoners who have trekked to this corner of South London to hunt out Smokey Jerkey. That voice, Louie, known as "Smokey" or "Jerkey" by regulars, has been at the helm of the shop since opening its doors in 2005.

On the same road that in 1981 saw over one thousand people march in protest against the infamous New Cross House Fire. it was a fire in the premises that saw the shop's need to strip back to its bare bones and subsequently provided the impetus for the simplicity that Smokey Jerkey is highly regarded for today.

Louie suggests that in good time Smokey Jerkey may return to the various sides and array of dishes that Caribbean restaurants across the UK are known for, however none too few would bemoan if things stayed exactly the same as they have been. In block capital letters the menu's main dishes read simply as jerk chicken, jerk pork or jerk lamb - each served with a choice of salad and white rice or rice and peas.

Armed with decades of cooking knowledge from his roots in Portland, Jamaica, Louie exudes a level of craft and dedication to jerk chicken usually reserved for Michelin starred sushi chefs. Here, on a daily basis Louie and the team commit to an unwavering schedule of seasoning, chopping and grilling on specially sourced charcoal. As a native of Portland, which is home to Boston Bay, the pronounced "Origin of Jerk" and former home to the annual Portland Jerk Festival (now hosted in Port Antonio, Portland,) Louie claims "jerkin" is in his blood.

With a career in carpentry, his expertise and lifelong interest in wood and foraging around the hills and bays of his homeland has found the perfect means of productivity in the food world. "Back when I was a yout, when I was hungry, I used to chip my dad's tree and use the piles to help cook me a pot of food!" recalls a grinning Louie. "In them days too our neighbour had some nice sarsaparilla and breadfruit plants and sometimes I used to quickly try and dig some up to cook with. The thing is, the more you dug them plants then the more they bared so it was all good."

"You can find anything for anything out there," Louie adds, "if you find some pimento, mature purple ones and mix with rum then you have Bay Rum and that's the Real McCoy – that can cure anyting!" Whilst no longer foraging across the plains of Jamaica, such a storied interest lives on in his jerk seasoning and an unassuming hot pepper sauce that sits atop the counter. "I call that one Scorpion sauce. It's from cayenne pepper but we call them bird peppers," he says, "If you never had it before it'll blow your top!"

Although many distant Londoners would love Louie to expand his operation closer to their neck of the woods, unfortunately for them he has grander plans at hand, "I want Smokey Jerkey across Africa," he proudly announces. "Sierra Leone and we start from there."

Kaieteur Kitchen
Elephant and Castle, S London

Faye Gomes sits at the literal cusp of change in the South London area of Elephant & Castle. Existing on the fringes of London's zone 1 transport area, her current stall lives underneath the famous shopping centre with its renowned Elephant & Castle statue that is amongst the last standing relics of a fading time. In the shadows of the increasingly looming array of skyscrapers and tower blocks Faye endeavours to carry on serving the people of the area her tenured Guyanese cooking at her Kaieteur Kitchen stall.

Opened in 2004, Faye describes, "a lot of things were here when I started." The shopping centre above currently operates at a fraction of its previous capacity and the office block above it that once provided her with streams of customers has declined even more so. After arriving in South London in 1992 from Buxton, a small village on the east coast region of the country once known as Demerara she did what she knew best - cooking.

"Cooking was always a part of my life" Faye reminisces. She waxes lyrical about a time Caribbean elders would make the youngers cook. Such was the case for Faye, "especially in the countryside" she adds. "Even during the week your older sister will call to make you stand and watch. How to make cake, how to peel fish" and so on. This turned into a passion and burgeoning career for Faye cooking and catering back in Guyana. Faye recalls, "'Back then you'd hardly ever find Guyanese food. Always Jamaican." Coming to London, a place that then and still now has a huge paucity of Guyanese food options there was nothing else that Faye was likely to do. When the Elephant and Castle unit was for sale from a fellow Guyanese wanting to move on, she jumped at the chance.

Faye, like many others hailing from Guyana explains how Guyana is a deeply diverse region known for its six races that all live side by side in each village including her own. Guyana is a melting pot of Africans, Indians, South Americans and Chinese so her current location here seems fitting with South London being home to dense populations of all those represented back in Guyana. Faye credits this diversity of her homeland for the popularity of her food and the diversity of her clients.

While some foods may seem different or have different names Faye explains how they're all related at the core. "What we call pholouri" the small fried spiced dough balls in India they may know them as pakora or pea balls." Continuing on she adds, "What the Jamaicans call dumplings we call bakes" and so the comparisons flow. "People are receptive", Faye recounts, "especially vegetarians as the Indian influence means a lot of veggie food." This is exemplified by the appearance of numerous vegetable curries laden with spinach, chickpeas, coconut sauce, beans and tomato sauce, which are staples all over the world.

The full menu is a prime case study in the global movement of food. There's of course fried plantain, a rich cassareep-based Pepper pot that is often served with Spanish rice and a selection of Chow Mein that are perhaps more of a favourite in Guyana then they are in the U.K. For the daring there are also links of Black pudding front and centre of the display. The eastern Caribbean shores are also much lauded for their sweet tooth, the possible result of a much larger Indian population than the west. This is thankfully catered for here with a host of simple baked sweet rolls and buns infused with shredded coconut and fruit.

The main unifier here however is the soft chickpea filled roti flatbread, handmade and homemade by Faye's own niece. Generously topped with the vegetable curries or myriad of meat dishes partnered with some chilli sauce is something that people from anywhere can comprehend and judging by the diverse clientele of the stall, clearly love. Faye says she "loves to explain Guyanese culture to people and how Guyanese products like coconut and cassava have so much utility" beyond just eating. The nation would be proud to know it had such a staunch flagbearer on these shores.

True Flavours

Acre Lane, SW London

First timers on south London's Acre Lane might be intrigued by the hustle and bustle constantly emanating out of one particularly shop regardless of the time of day, be it 10am or 10pm. That place, True Flavours, since opening has become a runaway hit on the lengthy stretch of road between south London's Brixton and Clapham areas. On the same road as the legendary Supertone Record store, True Flavours also joins good company being located next door to a convenience store now housed as a Costcutter newsagent, known to locals as "Cliffs" - one of the oldest Caribbean-owned general stores remaining in the country.

Far from the first to do Caribbean inspired food in the area, head chef and owner "Junior" depicts his two-decade veteran chef status in the area, "I've been cooking for a long time around here at a bunch of different restaurants and now people know me around here, and they know my cooking!" Making a daily commute to the kitchen every day at around 6am, Junior's passion for cooking over these years is unwavering. "Everyone in my family does this," adds Junior, "My family has always been fully involved in food, especially my mother and now my sister who runs a restaurant in Kellits, Clarendon called Falcon Crest."

When it comes to the constant energy on display at True Flavours, from both customers and staff, Junior praises a natural means of growth, "Word of mouth is simply the best advert to reaching out to other communities," he adds. It's no wonder then that word of mouth has spread such, the majority of the premises is dedicated to the rear kitchen rather than the front of house. With heavy pulsating Bashment music, the movement by hardworking co-chefs and attendants almost resembles a party, though the many customers who only know the multi-coloured beads on the other side of the shop's division may not know this.

Junior, who fosters this party spirit as much as the rest, very much channels this spirit into his food. Word of mouth, often regarding the vitality of True Flavours travels far, is usually reserved for Junior's cooking. When pressed as to what a first timer should go for Junior gleefully responds, "My Peppered Steak!" Junior's technique of slow-cooked simmered steak accompanied by chillies and a synthesis of spices in a classic Jamaica Sun Dutchpot may have even influenced the namesake of the restaurant. Whilst the oven tops are aligned with several of these pots, the darkest and most antique-looking one is reserved for the steak. Topped off with a sprig of herbs, it is then served with a choice of rice.

Perhaps akin to a parent picking out a their favourite offspring, it's hard for Junior to pick out a specific next preference but the golden fried fish cooked with precision as to walk the fine line between a fine crisp exterior and juicy interior stands out. For some who can't choose between the two an "off-the-board" Surf and Turf option (pictured next page) has become a winner.

With the decline of many of the area's record shops and social clubs, its clear True Flavours has become more than just a takeaway for the people in surroundings. Friends, family, old acquaintances and even motorbike enthusiasts alike all congregate and the cosiness of the shop's front of house almost propels you into someone else's conversation if you weren't having one of your own already. With some of Junior's earliest memories of Caribbean eateries in the area such as Lick Finger on the nearby Effra Road, now no longer in existence he has at least ensured an amusing social hub for the next generation to come.

People's Choice
Lower Clapton, E London

While it hasn't been around as long as the local street market which has existed in some format in the area since the 1930s, People's Choice emits the feeling that it has existed just off Chatsworth Road in East London's, Hackney for decades. The lead behind it owner and cook Leonard (Lenny), who earned his stripes manning the kitchen at Control Tower (p.98) for many years in the early 2000s after permanently making the move across the Atlantic from Jamaica in 1999. Lenny recalls good times there learning the business tips and tricks to running a whole kitchen, supplementing skills he had been crafting since he was a 12 year old boy in Jamaica's Cockburn Pen, Kingston.

Though, after branching out on his own, he recalls, "It wasn't easy man!" Lamenting the struggles of starting up any food based business endeavour. He nearly succumbed to a quiet resignation a few years after creating People's Choice in 2010. However, with staunch persistence, boundless assistance from wife Lorraine and after what he describes as a completely chance pickup of a steel jerk drum (now firmly placed outside the front of shop rain or shine), the drifting jerk smells started to attract local residents and those wondering down the long road between Clapton and Homerton, many of which now swear wholeheartedly by.

"After that things really changed," says Lenny and his serene process has since become a daily ritual. The process of Lenny's two hour slow cooked jerk chicken begins early in the morning long before the jerk is ready at around 11am, Lenny can be seen applying charcoal to the jerk drum and patiently waiting for it to heat before applying a number of succulent pieces of meat to the grill. While routinely opening up the barrel to let smoke escape, in between the hours it takes for the chicken to become a fine concoction of crisp jerk skin that retains a moist and juicy interior, Lenny is back and forth in the kitchen with Lorraine prepping up the meals of the day.

"That's why we're called People's Choice. We have to do a lickle something for everyone," he eludes, pointing to the days many offerings that are on full visibility from well outside the shop. Fluffy golden fried dumplings and sweet cornflour based festival dumplings rest in wait next to trays of green callaloo, luminous yellow plantain and ackee dotted with red peppers. This assortment of colours is no accident and you only have to look at Lenny's well-admired Rasta headwear and numerous accessories to realise this.

JB's
Peckham, SE London

JB's Soul Food & Fried Chicken, so named because of husband and wife duo Jennifer and Bill's passion for Caribbean cuisine, sits just off the high street of Peckham in South London. Although a relatively recent addition to the Peckham area in 2014, both Jennifer and Bill Hawes have been local residents for over twenty years since coming to the area in the early 1990s.

Hailing from Jamaica's capital Kingston, this pride makes the shop exceptionally hard to miss due to Bill's handy paintwork of the shop matching the Jamaican nation's gold and green motif. This bold colour scheme illuminates JB's aim to keep all aspects of the shop as authentically Jamaican as possible from the outside façade to all the way inside the kitchen.

A mechanic and technician by trade, Bill's steel barrel drum, designed and built with nothing but a mental diagram aided by years of experience has become a local institution and made their jerk chicken a crowd pleaser from the early hours of the morning to the late hours of the night. Bill recounts a common refrain from many of those well versed in cooking and eating Jerk Chicken – that it can't be real jerk if it is not cooked in a steel drum.

On any given day the couple can be seen working in tandem, with Bill transporting several of his tubs of previously prepared special jerk seasoning, carefully marinating every crevice of the pre-grilled chicken, whilst Jen, leaning on her childhood experiences cooking alongside her mother, heads the front of house serving up everything from patties, peppered steak, curried chicken, and even their own trademark of sweet chilli wings. All this with a welcoming aura. For novice Caribbean food enthusiasts, JB's has developed their own mini range to help introduce people to the more exotic worlds of goat and oxtail.

With locally sourced meat often coming from the nearby Dennis' Butchers (p.58) and a variety of supplemental ingredients coming from the many local stores and market vendors in Peckham synonymous with the area's Afro-Caribbean community, the pair go to an extra length for a certain level of quality and authenticity preferring to use a select few ingredients straight from their native Jamaica. A flourishing instance of this culmination is JB's "weekend only" smoke infused jerk pork, leaving many to clamour for it during the seemingly long week without it.

Whilst currently holding back on the inclination to multiply their operation, for the moment, their range of homespun juices featuring the creamy, nutmeg seasoned Guinness punch and a ginger and citrus laden carrot juice satisfies customers need for expansion.

Previously the edge of a neglected road, where the TV show "Youngers" was filmed depicting the trials and tribulations for youth in Southeast London, times have much changed in the area and JB's has swiftly added a touch of vitality to a once dormant road becoming a local hotspot from sunrise to long after sunset.

JB's Soul Food Menu

Patties £1.30

	Small	Large
Jerk chicken + Rice	£5.00	£6.00
Brown Stew chicken + Rice	£5.00	£6.00
Curry chicken + Rice	£5.00	£6.00
Curry Goat + Rice	£5.50	£6.50
Oxtail + Rice	£6.00	£7.00
Fish + Rice	£6.00	£7.00
Hard Food + meat	£6.00	£7.00
Ackee + Saltfish	£6.00	£7.50
Callaloo + Saltfish	£5.00	£6.50
Jerk Pork + Rice (Fridays + Saturdays)	£6.00	£7.00

Soup of the Day!
any soup
£2.50 small £3.00 large

Friday and Saturday!
Jerk Pork
£5 per portion

Cakes - £1.50 per slice
steamed vegetables - £2

Jerk chicken

Zionly Food Hall

Peckham, SE London

The word Ital, has its origins in the English word vital hence, the rhyming catchphrase Ital is Vital! Known across Jamaica and further afield, the term Ital has its foundations rooted in Rastafarianism, a now worldwide social movement, religious group and mindset of people following the rites of former Ethiopian ruler, and King of Kings, Haile Selassie. Within the creed there are many cultural divisions and beliefs. However, most tenets stem from the word of the First Testament in the Christian Holy Bible.

Given this, there exists an abundance of discord about what exactly constitutes Ital food but the basis remains an ethos of pure, natural foods from the Earth, free of additives and chemicals commonplace in modern food. Taking certain passages of the Holy Bible about the treatment of self and all of Jah's (God) creatures literally this has also ruled out the consumption of all meat produce, especially that stemming from pork.

When long tenured south London resident Jason (Jahson) Peat was introduced to these ideas many years ago as well as the wider pan-African ideology that encompassed them he began a journey to share them with the people of the UK. With his entrepreneurial spirit he started a string of businesses across South London. He initially was primarily based in Brixton where he thrived until rents quadrupled to a point that was beyond sustainability for his enterprise.

An indoor arcade at the centre of nearby south London Peckham's bustling Rye Lane has formed the home of Jahson's latest venture Zionly Food Hall. To understand Zionly, it is better to understand Jahson as an educator or teacher rather than just a cook or restaurateur (which he is great). He's had previous endeavours in the arts and crafts and the now gone but much revered bookstore next door that housed books on a whole spectrum of genres from African culture, history, religion and spirituality. Whether its food, the arts or teaching traditional drumming at local schools, the quest is to aid the goal of reframing the external vision of the pan-African world to the diaspora themselves and to the wider world.

The concentration however, at this very time is food. Jahson waxes lyrical about the natural Rastafari lifestyle espousing the idea that prevention is better than healing. You'll be hard pressed to find a set menu of any kind. Rather a set ideology. Everything is cooked on the same morning before opening. Food is sourced from the very same local markets you see on the way to the arcade providing uniqueness and freshness that moves with the local times. You may not find the typical Afro-Caribbean fare here, instead a daily roster that utilises things that are plentiful in the tropical world showing the possibilities and expanding the horizons of what can emanate from the pan-African world. Existing outside this rigid niche also admittedly helps appeal equally to the local Caribbean population as well as the new growing global cohort of local residents.

On this particular day mixed couscous and kale dominated greens options are served alongside red peas stew with sweet potato and stir fry pasta with mushrooms. Other dishes served here include curry mushy peas, peanut butter stew, spinach and butternut squash in addition to red lentils and sweet potato curry. On the more experimental of days delights such as Shepherd's pie are filled with the flavoursome Rastafari spirit. While the menu changes daily, some things are a daily fixture due to popular demand of which the exemplar is the spinach infused wholemeal fried dumplings. Whichever day is chosen, expect a visually exciting experience with prices that Jahson's considers at a point that can deter people from the frequent visits to the growing amount of fast food outlets in the nearby area.

While the principles of health will continue to underpin the ethos of Zionly, peat believes there is a way to offer meat and fish done in the healthiest way possible, instigating the shift from the vegan Zionly Manna outfit to Zionly Food Hall. It is also a way to cleverly branch out to a broader audience and bring them into the fold where they can then try the wealth of food and be brought under the wing of Jahson's education.

Jahson's and his tied locs coronet can often be seen bopping up and down Rye Lane frequently being hailed by past patrons, friends and acquaintances alike indicating his presence in the community as more than just a vendor. Jahson is an ideas man and constantly looking at ways to improve and enlighten the local community.

Caribbean Kitchen

Hackney, E London

Since the late 1940s into the 1950s, after the World Wars, the London borough of Hackney has been home to a more than substantial Caribbean community. At the heart of this borough on Mare Street sits the Empire theatre, borough Town Hall and central library in succession, which have all been pivotal resources and centres for the Caribbean as various other global migrant groups that all reside in close proximity with each other. Down the far end of the road towards the neighbouring borough of Tower Hamlets sits Caribbean Kitchen, that is keeping the legacy of this Caribbean community alive as one of the handful of Caribbean businesses left on the street.

The humble food space was started by couple Ann-Marie and Rohan Griffiths in 2013 after they noticed an empty shop front in a state of disrepair. It was love at first sight and the couple immediately saw the potential in the premises. They pulled together a few family and friends to renovate and refurbish the premises and their new restaurant, Cafe Heath, so called after the nearby Cambridge Heath locale and railway station was born in late 2013.

The space saw the couple experiment with various iterations. Ultimately, owing to the pair's mixed Caribbean heritage (Ann-Marie descending from Jamaica and Rohan from Antigua and Jamaica) they settled on the idea of Caribbean Kitchen. Previously a more formal setting they eventually evolved into the canteen style space that the local community and beyond has grown to love.

For head chef Ann-Marie, being born and raised in Jamaica, the islands' food was part of her DNA and the opportunity to share it with a wider British audience was too good to pass. She strives to infuse authentic Jamaican flavours in all the dishes she prepares. The ranges from classics like boneless stewed beef or chicken, succulent jerk chicken and curry goat. At the end of the working week, in true Caribbean fashion expect incredible seafood Fridays with bespoke platters laden with choices of muscle, prawns, crabs' legs and lobster, boiled vegetables and fruit. On the veggie side of things, they've perfected a chickpea and sweet potato curry that has proven to have mass appeal with people from all walks of life.

For afters, there are an ever-alternating roster of baked goods and cakes illustrating the variety and depth of Caribbean cuisine be it the vegan hemp seed & banana loaf or the Guinness & chocolate cake. In addition to this, whilst there are a host of island favourite soft drinks on offer the kitchen ensures there are some healthy but tasty drinks in the form of home-made Sorrel drink made from hibiscus and compounded with ginger as well as ital moss drink made from soaked seaweed and organic flax seed.

The underpinning of the business has always been that they "believe in preparing food with love from the heart which will bring people and cultures together." With this, keeping true to their roots has forged a fanbase that has rapidly brought them towards this goal. Rather than some fancy artwork Ann-Marie describes that she wanted some sort of homage to this and so they opted to have a whole entire wall as a guestbook of sorts for their streams of patrons. Hand-written signatures and heartfelt messages from customers hailing from all corners of the world are a real testament to the effectiveness of small businesses like Caribbean Kitchen to introduce people to forge cultural exchanges and relations.

The couple's original dream was to bring back the light heartiness and welcoming approach of the owners of a Caribbean Restaurant, and all its staff that Ann-Marie ensures are predominantly women from the local area who are all well versed in Caribbean food no matter their own heritage. The effect of this warm service is evident with people travelling from all across London to visit and the increasing number of Caribbean Kitchen star-studded catering gigs.

Bokit'la

London

The majority of Caribbean diaspora in the UK hail from Jamaica, which often means that Jamaican culture often supplants the cultures of other islands. With this, the traditions and of course the food from other islands are often overlooked. For members of the French Caribbean community descending from Martinique and Guadeloupe, the language barrier resulting from their French colonial heritage puts them even more of a step back in the UK's Caribbean pecking order.

Guadeloupe-born brothers, Nicolas (Nico) and Thierry Baptiste of the exciting street food and catering outfit Bokit'la are on a mission to change this. Since coming to the UK in the late 1990s and after a decade living without some of their favourite comfort foods, the pair knew something had to be done about it.

Their vision was, "for us to finally have French Caribbean food in London." Assessing the burgeoning street food scene at the time around 2011, there was a number of Guadeloupean foods they could have forged a name with but ultimately, as Nico describes, "we though it of bokits because it is popular back home and we thought it would be a no brainer to introduce this one because back home we loved it."

In the 1600s, French forces brought west African slaves, along with European produce and Asian spices to Guadeloupe and the island formed the calabash of cultures seen today. The story so goes that the snack originally named "boukit" was inspired by the "Johnny Cake" which is a kind of fried bread that the New England colonies in turn potentially may have borrowed (using that term liberally) from the original Amerindian tribes of the island.

Save for some additional spices, the base ingredients, like the fried dumplings of Jamaica, were simply flour, water and salt. After the abolishment of the slave trade and emancipation many freed slaves and islanders were plunged into generational poverty and subsisted on what food they could afford to make. Hence, the bokit become a staple snack.

Many years later, this same simplicity is the root of the Baptiste's choice to form their business around the bokit snack. As Nico describes, "it's basically a freshly baked dough, deep fried. Our dough is light but some other islands make it thicker, a bit heavier but we chose to do ours a bit more light and hollow and not so heavy on the belly" compared to the likes of the sometimes sleep inducing fried dumpling sandwiches popular in Jamaica and Shark bakes popular in the likes of Trinidad and Guyana.

Utilising this simple canvas, Bokit'la manages to stuff a world of flavours into these hot pockets. The primary mainstays here are grilled chicken and flaming hot pan cooked saltfish cut up into small succulent pieces. For the vegans, there's also an option of smooth, cooked down aubergine accompanied by liberal amounts of avocado. This is something less likely to be seen on the streets of Basse-Terre, the Guadeloupe capital but as Nico details, "There's a lot of vegans in London so we created this filling for them because usually you don't find that at home."

The fun doesn't end there. Another island favourite accras, a round ball form of the saltfish fritter more popular on the Easterly shores of the Caribbean comes as a standalone snack but somehow the sandwich can be neatly fissured to make room for them.

After all this, you are compelled into picking a hot chilli sauce ranging from level one being mild to level five extra hot. Nico tells, "we also have an incredible creole chilli sauce made by our mother Yolande" who is described by the team as a scientist spice master. He continues "She thought of doing a different level of spice so that everyone can spice up their food." If the hot sauce gets too much for you their sweet and flavourful caress juice fruit punch is there to save the day.

Bokit'la fits all the criteria for a perfect metropolis street food scene. The sandwiches are moreish, portable, and have an endless array of combinations. In addition to their food, the jovial nature of the crew can often be seen combining cooking with vibrant bops to Soca and Dancehall music emanating from their speakers. This has led to the crew being in demand across London with constant shouts online for them to expand. Nico happily advocates, "If you want to know about French Caribbean food and have something different, we recommend that you come and try our food."

Mama's Jerk

London

While the Mama's Jerk that London and the UK. has grown to know and love has been in existence since 2010, the roots of the business lie almost a century back in the centrally located town of Mandeville in Jamaica. Here, lay the farmhouse that was the home of Mama's Jerk founder Adrian Luckie's great grandmother Mama Charlotte. "She was called Mama by everyone in town." Adrian recalls. Hence the outfits name was an easy choice.

In this rural setting, she developed a jerk recipe, the contents of which are kept under tight seal.

As, Adrian describes, "Mama's Jerk barbecue marinade recipe was originally made by my late Nan." Adding, "it was while she was experimenting that she created her secret recipe in her old farmhouse back-a-yard kitchen." In true trial and testing fashion, "Mama Charlotte used to grow all her fresh ingredients for her recipes on her farm, after gathering them she began mashing and mixing them to create her own secret recipe of the Jamaican classic, jerk barbecue marinade for the jerk chicken and jerk pork dishes."

This jerk barbecue marinade was so tasty, as is told that she could put it on anything. Fortunately, for the people of the UK, she not only passed the recipe down the generations but she also encouraged her many children and grandchildren to experiment with, and venerate food.

Adrian tells, "she created so many wonderful Caribbean flavours that brings back fond memories of barbecue's round the back a yard fire." After being immersed in this heritage amongst the densely Caribbean diaspora domain of South London, it was a no-brainer that Adrian would follow in these footsteps to keep these memories alive.

Mama's Jerk was set up in March 2009 by Adrian to try and create a legacy for Mama's secret jerk barbecue Sauce recipe. This led him venturing out on his own to start a Caribbean street food business striving to be different. To achieve this the plan was to simplify the jerk product in the form of jerk chicken wraps. Starting at the legendary Vibe Bar on Brick Lane in East London with scores of loyal fans they were able to build up a platform to be where they are today growing a small empire of Mama's Jerk.

Adrian states, "We like to try differentiating ourselves from other West Indian takeaways restaurants with the food we produce, service we provide and style branding of our operations. We are not afraid to try fusing classic dishes like jerk lamb shank with sweet potato mash and jerk gravy or creating gluten-free, vegan and vegetarian dishes. We will try to mainly focus on healthy clean eating."

This fearlessness has been the impetus for many Mama's Jerk dishes that you'll be hard pressed to find anywhere else such as the Biriyardi their version of the classic biryani, their jerk seasoned rice and peas are mixed with sweetcorn and plantain and served with their 24-hour marinated jerk chicken and jerk spiced saltfish cakes. As Mama Jerk's jests, "Mama doesn't let her Veggie Jerks down," and judging by the popularity of their jerk veggie bean cake wraps this is clear to see. A magical composition of sweet potato, kidney beans, black eyed peas, coconut, plantain, thyme, parsley and of course Mama's secret Jerk Marinade, all finished off in natural breadcrumbs do well to highlight the meat-free vibrancy of Caribbean produce.

This reflexiveness has put Mama's Jerk in good stead for the future as Adrian surmises, "Caribbean food is growing and the opportunities coming their own give motivation to keep going."

... Q
...gs £6.⁵⁰

Jerk Burgers £8.⁹⁵

A COCOBUN BURGER WITH A CHOICE OF

JERK BBQ CHICKEN BURGER

— OR —

JERK SPICED VEGAN BEANCAKE BURGER

— OR —

JERK SPICED SALTFISH CAKE BURGER

JERK BBQ SAUCE – MANGO MAYO
HOT PEPPER PICKLE £0.30

Side Tings

JERK SPICED FRIES £3

—

PLAIN FRIES £3

—

FRIED PLANTAIN £3

—

PICKLED SLAW £2

Jerk Biriy...

RICE & PEAS MEAL W...

JERK BBQ CHIC...

— OR —

JERK SPIC...

JERK BBQ SAUCE ...
HOT PEPPER P...

MAMA'S JERK

www.mama...station.com

Jamaica Patty Co.

Covent Garden, London

With a lifelong dedication to promoting Jamaican culture across the world, it seemed inevitable that Theresa Roberts would make a foray into the food world given the Caribbean's rich and diverse cuisine history. Alongside husband Andrew, the pair have taken this diversity, embedded with a sense of British heritage and paired it with the sensibilities of a fast paced commerce environment common to their central London surroundings.

With Andrew being born and raised in Falmouth, Cornwall – the birthplace of the Cornish Pasty, the emphasis on the patty seemed like destiny. After moving to Southwest London from the serene agricultural landscape of Black River, St Elizabeth in Jamaica as a young girl, Theresa admittedly faced a culture shock and found it tough adjusting to British food. With this, she found solace in the Caribbean influenced home cooking of her parents. This background influenced her estimation of the potential of her island's food and some years into the future, not entirely satisfied with the quality and diversity of patty offerings in the nation's capital, Theresa and husband invested in the country's focal snack. The difference however would be the inclusion of high quality ingredients and a forward facing brand that could help take the food and Caribbean culture to an international audience.

Having conceived and self-designed every microscopic element of the store, Theresa's Jamaican background shows itself in various facets throughout. "In Jamaica, my first school was under a palm tree! We were educated under a tree in the shade." However, Theresa's vision of the store was not Palm Trees and so forth but simply the essence of that terrain, giving a modern outlook and brand to her native country. Theresa adds, "I always wanted to show the world what a good quality product Jamaica has to offer."

This doesn't just stem to her own creation in JPC but also the introduction to central London of various storied Jamaican Brands such as Grace Kennedy plantain crisps, the famous Devon House "I-Scream" Ice Cream, (produced under license in the UK by a small family business specialising in sourcing the creamiest milk) and four flavours of Tortuga Rum Cake (golden original, Blue Mountain coffee, chocolate and coconut) which are imported directly from the Tortuga Bakery in Montego Bay. This, along with the founding inclusion of Jamaican chef Collin Brown to help develop the patties all provides a system of fostering growth in Jamaican business and provide Londoners with a "True Jamaican experience" that Theresa holds in high esteem.

The experience doesn't end there however, always striving to incorporate more "Jamaicaness," JPC's own brand of Blue Mountain coffee, "The Best Coffee in the world," with a regional label that matches France's champagne is imported to the UK in green bean form but roasted here to ensure a real taste of freshness. The underlying philosophy here remains Theresa's passion of introducing people from all walks of life to Caribbean and Jamaican culture in particular. Whether that's fine art from the island, paying homage to her fathers music taste with the likes of John Holt soothing the shop's airwaves and of course the patties. Whilst the beef, veggie, curried goat and saltfish n' ackee patties are all crowd pleasers, Theresa admits, "For newcomers I always suggest the jerk chicken of course!"

Eat of Eden

London

When Eat of Eden's colourful mountainous plates of goodness arrived at Brixton's the village they took the local populace by storm. Save for a handful of Ital Rastafari led outposts, the presence and awareness of afro-veganism was scarce on the high streets of the UK. At a moment in time when the image of veganism was becoming somewhat homogenised across the country, the first humble outpost of Eat of Eden located in South London's Brixton helped affect a change in the meat abstaining scene. It also served a purpose of raising awareness to the long-time centuries old presence of veganism in the pan-African world.

Eat of Eden aims "to inspire vegans to be creative with the taste and presentation of plant-based food." The outfit describe their menus as inspired by Caribbean Ital and European recipes and they have quickly become masters at taking what culinary ideas London knows and understand and reproducing them in a vibrant manner. The burgers with fillings varying from spicy bean to Barbecued seitan and caramelised mushroom all serve this purpose in introducing new flavours people may not have tried in a vehicle they can comprehend.

The same goes for Ital patties. Many in the UKs numerous migrant populated metropolises may have been fortunate to try a Caribbean baked pattie at some point in their life. Here, the popular street snack is reimagined in vegan form while a wholemeal, dairy free shell that again houses an explosion of tastes be it the mixed vegetables flavour, the callaloo edition or a very rare dal lentil filling that you'll be hard pressed to find at any other outpost.

The star of the show however are the magical DIY platters that come in a variety of sizes. There is nothing actually mini about the mini platter that could fill up even the hungriest of punters except its size compared the sharing platter clocking up a behemoth option of twelve items. Beyond usual pulse fare of white rice or rice and peas Eat of Eden broadens the plate fillers with selections such as bulgur wheat, quinoa and even black rice. These are liberally accompanied by the likes of chickpea or pumpkin and sweet potato curry. The more typical Caribbean extras such as plantain, macaroni n' cheese make a welcome appearance as well as lesser known Eat of Eden creations such as seaweed fritters and meat emulating barbecued seitan.

The inventions don't stop at food. All meals are handily washed down with an assortment of health-conscious drinks such as sea moss fused with Afro-Caribbean health mainstays like spirulina as well as takes on Caribbean classics like Guinness punch, here made with almond milk rather than the regular condensed milk or vanilla energy drinks. Following timeless advice from the Rastafari and more recently the teachings from the likes of Dr. Sebi, a focus is also placed on the importance of Alkaline water helping to neutralise the acidity of the modern diet.

The recent expansion of the collective across London suggests people are increasingly receptive to the diversity of veganism and through this the legacy of Ital food (p.199) can hopefully live on.

The Globe
Notting Hill, W London

In the 1960s, author and broadcast journalist Mike Phillips once recounted of West London's dwindling Notting Hill area, "'It was the Caribbean immigrants who took hold of Notting Hill, and ironically gave it its contemporary character…" Hence, with most of the existing social establishments proving unwelcoming to the newly arrived population, many of the new influx of residents developed their own collective scene consisting of various types of social hubs. There were after-hours drinking clubs, basement/cellar-clubs for daytime gambling, rent parties, and underground cafés.

In 1958 around 7000 migrants had settled in the area around Colville Terrace, which was often dubbed 'Brown Town' as opposed to the nearby White City. This era proved to be a turbulent era for the incoming community, culminating in the Notting Hill race riots, which arguably provided the impetus for Notting Hill Carnival. With this, where the likes of Totobag's Café on Blenheim Crescent and the Calypso Club on Westbourne Terrace have now long perished, amongst the last physical remnants of this era in Notting Hill is The Globe Bar on Talbot Road. Over the years, in spite of the bar changing ownership has always endeavoured to retain as much of the original façade as possible both inside and out.

Being next door to one of the of the area's first underground clubs in the basement of Fullerton's Tailors on Talbot Road (where legendary Jamaican-born DJ Duke Vin was the selector), the origins of The Globe bar date back to the 1950s. In its current guise however, The Globe identity was founded by pioneering black actor Roy Stewart, who also ran an all-inclusive gym nearby at 32a Powis Square that had been set up even before the riots in 1958. The renowned body-builder and actor of the times, Stewart appeared in the James Bond films 'Dr No' and 'Live and Let Die', the Rolling Stones' 'One Plus One (Sympathy for the Devil)', 'Leo the Last' (on the site of Lancaster West estate) and many 'Carry On' films.

In the midst of the "Swinging Sixties" era, which has been enshrined in West London's cultural legacy, The Globe became a hotspot for the who's who in the worlds of art, fashion and music. The bar was habitually famously frequented by the likes of rock n' roll legends The Beatles, The Rolling Stones, Jimi Hendrix and Van Morrison as a place for after-parties or often just as a hangout spot throughout the week. Hendrix himself was reputedly last seen there the night he passed away in 1970. Not just an after-hours bar and club, the upstairs was, and still is, known for its late night restaurant with then members of newly migrated Caribbean community heading up the kitchen.

With its weekly parties and host of in-house popup restaurants, The Globe remains a popular late night destination for the ever-changing community of West London. Enjoying a plate of rice n peas or shaking a leg until the early hours of the morning is a guaranteed way to ensure for many to say they followed in the footsteps of Bob Marley.

OVER SIXTIES NIGHT

At the **GLOBE** 12 - 4pm

FOOD & DRINKS HALF PRICE

Old time classics from the 20's

Tel:020 7221 0652

MEMBERS ONLY AFTER 7pm

.OBE

GLOBE
RESTAURANT
OPEN TO ALL
BASEMENT CLUB
MEMBERS & GUESTS ONLY

RACING

HI-LO Jamaican Eating House

Cowley Road, Oxford

As one of first bar-restaurants on Cowley Road, the road that links the automotive industrial estate of Oxford down toward the gothic spires of the city's University, Hi-Lo "Jamaican Eating House & Take Away" has been a legendary hangout spot for both town locals and university students since its inception in 1979.

Coming to England as a teenager, Hi-Lo founder, Hugh "Andy" Anderson embarked on a career studying and working in electronics across England's West Country, Yorkshire district and London working with the BBC and a number of other organisations for a number of years. Following this, after some years Andy and family settled down in the quieter city of Oxford, about half way between London and Bristol.

This was an area that Andy had become somewhat familiar with by that time. "There wasn't nothing else on this road back then!" proclaimed Andy, recalling just a handful of restaurants. Longing for a style of Shebeen bar that had become especially popular with those back home, he strived to create a place in Oxford that would not only serve dishes reminiscent of his hometown of Clarendon in Jamaica but a place that would also serve the finest selection of rum and Dragon Stout into the early hours of the morning when many of the nearby pubs and social spaces had long retired.

With a self-built DJ booth tucked away near the front restaurant that houses a vintage steel turntable and stacks upon stacks of vinyl dubs that he has collected over the years, Andy was more able to "Control the

vibes" in Hi-Lo as he puts it. This also helped extend Hi-Lo's appeal, as it became a popular dance function venue that over years was home to like of the infamous Trojan sound system and more recently Oxford's Skylarkin sound system. As the numerous hanging homages to esteemed Jazz and Reggae artists and colossal speakers dotted around Hi-Lo attest, music has always been at the heart of the establishment. This passion led Andy and local friends to start the first Caribbean Carnival in South Parks, amongst a wide number of other parties in the region throughout the times.

Long before the numerous fried chicken, kebab and pizza places dotted along the entirety of Cowley Road there was limited opportunity to grab a late night meal in the area, let alone a meal befitting an entire Caribbean family. With Andy gracing the luminous neon bar pouring up pints of Guinness and Red Stripe, wife Jan can be found back and forth between the back of house serving up Hi-Lo's infamous "Funky Chicken" and a range of other main courses including snapper fish, jerk chicken and a selection of finely cooked pork. All served with a choice of Jan's decorative deft touch of plantain, fried breadfruit, avocado or melon.

Over the years, a chance late night stumble into Hi-Lo after 3am may have seen Andy having curry goat and a side of callaloo with many would be Prime Ministers and City Mayors in the decades to come. With Andy having no intention of stopping anytime soon, he contentedly awaits a friendly chat with those who continue to pass through.

Plantation Inn

Leytonstone, E London

Plantation Inn's homepage, laden with testimonials from numerous government and diplomatic officials, joyfully estimates how many dishes they have served in over three decades of service. 81,000 main dishes served, a total of over 98,000 accompaniments and over 31,000 deserts to round things up. All this suggests the prodigious tenure of Plantation Inn. In 1984, an era where opportunities for fine dining experiences for the swelling Caribbean community in London were scant, George and Mayblin Hamilton sought to bring something new to the table – A high end silver service experience combined with a menu reminiscent of life back home on the Caribbean islands.

"It was a lot more grey back then!" George exclaims. Numerous factories in the Waltham Forest borough of East London had, as they had across many parts of the UK, attracted migrants from across the Commonwealth to seek out employment. George tells, "I came to England when I was 17 on the 5th September 1974!" Having then navigated a boisterous career as a technical and mechanical engineer whilst simultaneously tending to his passion as a world touring gigging musician (mainly a bass guitar he still whips out on occasion) in the 1970s.

Already running his own enterprise in the Leyton area, George's attention turned to food, "There was hardly anywhere to get Caribbean food then, and we couldn't find anywhere to get dressed up and have a dinner with it. There were so few places for Caribbean people to enjoy a dinner," he tells. Following a trip to St. Lucia, inspired by the manner of service at the upmarket hotel restaurants and so forth, which exuded an air of luxury, George recalls how he found much inspiration.

After meeting with the Jamaican High Commission to formulate some ideas, in 1984 Plantation Inn began service with as George puts it "A big splash! We invited all the local mayors at the time - Hackney, Waltham Forest, Newham, Redbridge…All of them. We also got a lot of write ups from the likes of The Gleaner."

From there the rest was history. Those who enjoyed a refined take on the likes of curry goat or escovitch fish complemented with a rum bar, silk waist-coated attendees and a full live band immediately told friends and family. George recalls, "People came from all over! We did weddings over twenty years ago and people still remember me."

Working alongside wife Mayblin, who was the designated cook in a family of twelve, Plantation Inn was created to be, and remains a culmination of all the families' experiences. George reminisces, "My grandmother used to work on a plantation field so that provided inspiration for the name." A descendent of May Pen, in Jamaica's Clarendon, George also remembers visiting the area's famous Denbigh annual agricultural and food show, which from a very early age engrained food commerce in him. All this, cemented with a professional expertise gained from his industrial career held Plantation Inn in good stead from the start.

"After the service was up and running, people would always come in asking for takeaway," to which the restaurant eventually obliged. Both the restaurant and takeaway continued until the family had decided to wind down both by the mid 2000s and focus on catering, which had already been a winner across the country. Already serving Caribbean and foreign diplomats, the High Commission and Embassy, the restaurant had already cultivated a highly sophisticated outfit easily replicated at numerous birthdays, wakes, christenings, weddings and even for the 2012 Gold-winning Jamaican Olympic team.

With a keen eye for crystal clear glass, mirror clean cutlery and elegantly folded napery, George humorously eludes that he is still "fussy about presentation." Hence, a date with Plantation Inn in charge of the kitchen will always see Mr. Hamilton donned in a dapper suit and tie in the heart of the action.

Troy Bar
Shoreditch, E London

For over two decades, Troy Bar has been quietly nestled in the heart of East London's Shoreditch area providing locals and globetrotters alike with an eclectic array of sounds. Before the area became one of London's busiest hubs for revellers and late-night antics Eddie Charles' Troy Bar, almost like a Trojan horse, has been ferrying everything from soul, jazz, blues, funk, reggae and more into central London. With the bar placing just as much emphasis and importance on local debuting talent as it does on international superstars it quickly became known as the place to catch an incredible vibe on any night of the week.

Shoreditch, a place located Between the residential and highly diverse London borough of Hackney and the commercial hub of London's finance centre transformed in the last decade from a desolate strip into a metropolis. While few local and family owned businesses were able to survive the swell, Troy Bar's established acclaim kept it a people's favourite and go-to destination over years. As punters at Troy Bar often ate elsewhere before attending the bar saw the opportunity to incorporate the food of their heritage and something you couldn't get nearby into their offering and as such the Caribbean food became one of the bar's best kept secrets.

From the open mic sessions every Tuesday, it's legendary "Word of Mouth" jazz funk jam sessions on Friday night or perhaps it's midweek foray into finding the best in emerging live talent every night became known for something different and special. In addition, all these nights were spiced up with a plethora of drinks and authentic homemade Caribbean cuisine.

With a new string of devotees as equally fanatic about their food as they were the jazz it wasn't long until calls for the bar's food came during the day when the bar usually lay dormant, resting from the pulsating vibration of the night before. As the area's once baron building blocks and warehouses transformed into one of the creative hubs of not just London but all of Europe word of mouth about Troy Bar again quickly spread. To match the new scores of hungry mouths during Weekday lunchtimes the bar, with little fanfare opened doors and spread out its tables at lunchtime. The goal here was to provide those in the area with a flavoursome and comparatively very very reasonably priced alternative to the now growing amount of grab-and-go food chains in the area.

As they aren't a fully-fledged restaurant, the bar keeps its simple with just a handful of choices and as a result each is given due care and attention to detail. From the meat heavy curry goat, curry chicken and jerk chicken to the seafood options of grilled or steamed fish everyone has their favourite that they swear by. All are served with a choice of seasoned rice or rice and peas alongside sweet pieces of plantain, green salad and finished with coleslaw and curry sauce. With the queue often out the door, it's easy to see how the bumper plates have been successful in satiating everyone's hunger from lunch until home time.

The Honeypot
Brockley, SE London

Approaching two decades of business just off Brockley's Lewisham Way, between New Cross and the town centre of Lewisham in South London is The Honeypot. With a dining area adorned with silk flowers, floral table covers and adjacent kitchen with Dancehall music booming nearby, the place evokes true nostalgia of a West Indian household from generations past.

This homeliness has kept people driving from as far as Kent and beyond for all these years since the mid-1990s when the shop first opened its doors. Whilst the definitive Caribbean meals like the curried and stewed dishes have always assured custom, the BBQ jerk chicken stood out from the regular jerk chicken and small delicacies such as bammy (a cassava flatbread snack), sprats (small seasoned fish), liver n' kidney and cow foot were a delight for those used to such dishes from home as well as catching the interest of newcomers to the food.

Whilst The Honeypot at times during the course of a week is a bustling hub of jokes and chat, no other time of the week is this more prevalent than on Friday evenings when The Honeypot's famous Fish Fridays get into full swing. A concoction of locally sourced seafood from Billingsgate Market is turned, by specially brought-in chefs, into dazzling, mouthwatering display of dishes from fried and steamed fish to the elaborate crab and lobster platter arrangements. All of which are portioned with a kaleidoscopic array of prawns, fruits and vegetables. Whilst a few choose to dine-in, many are happy with the treasure chest of a silver tray that has become synonymous with the shop's Fish Friday.

As regulars pull up in their cars and joyously gather in the common opposite the shop, the space from the kitchen all the way out on to green became a guaranteed spot to catch up with old pals at the end of a long week.

Although the shop has changed hands over the years this history has been encapsulated across the walls of the shop in the dozens framed photos hanging on the wall. In the age of digital photography such a display of physical documentary has become rare and the fact they remain up after all these years speaks to how important The Honeypot has been to the local area. A deeper glance at the photos and it is clear that The Honeypot's Garlic and Pepper prawns have played a part in the development of some of England's superstar footballers and boxers who grew up in the local area.

Fish Friday

@ Honeypot

Lobster • Steam Fish
Fried Fish • Roast Fish
Garlic Prawns
Bami • Pepper Prawns
Seabottom Soup • Festival

Jamaican Ways

Radford, Nottingham

"Growing up learning how to survive," has been a key factor for Jamaican Ways owner-chef Richard Newland, in making his establishment Nottingham's now longest running Caribbean eating post. The history of the restaurant is embedded in Richard's background growing up in rural Springfield, a town in Clarendon to the south of Jamaica. "We used to plant our own vegetables, we had our own goats, we used to have to go down to the gully and fetch water ourselves, we'd even go to the woods and get wood for the fire… which we eventually used with the goats."

"I remember my grandma would give me 50 cents to get some bulla cake but I would get a bag of flour and make as many fried dumplings as I could instead! It was touch back then. I had to fend myself during the week when the family wasn't around." Having had to forage and cook for himself from the age of seven as a pure means of survival proved an indispensable foundation to the kind of experimentation observed in Jamaican Way's canteen service.

Richard recalls, "I remember at that young age I had a butter pan, and I used to go to dig around people's garden for yams which I used to make rundown." Across the Atlantic some years later after having completed numerous catering and professional chef qualifications, learning how to cross and fuse cuisines, his childhood notion of discovery still reigns supreme. For his creamy coconut based rundown dishes, Richard tells, "It took TEN years to find the perfect coconut milk but it was worth it!"

To Richard, the name Jamaican Ways represents a Jamaican way of doing things. As such, "Jamaica and the Caribbean in general are made up of so many different ethnicities - if you just limited yourself to a strictly native Jamaican cuisine the menu would be very limited." As an unabashed foodie, Richard regularly calls upon his extensive library of cookbooks from classical French to Mediterranean cuisine, Creole history and modern Caribbean food from all the different islands. "Birthdays are easy for me! Everyone just knows to get me a cookbook."

A key example for this is the rice entrée. Not content with just the standard rice & peas or white rice offering, Richard took inspiration from across the world to develop a callaloo rice rish, gumbo rice with chicken (featuring a few secret ingredients), pilau rice and an okra & brown lentil offering amongst many others. The menu is peppered with a magnitude of homages to the variety of global cultures that have piqued Richard's interest and in many ways are linked to the West Indies. A popular Caribbean "stir fry" for example, seasoned Yam balls harking back to the Caribbean's relationship with West Africa and even nostalgic references to a 20th Century British upbringing with Bakewell tarts and Madeira cake.

From the puffy roti bread, to the boneless effervescent coley fish, and even the creamy pea soup, all the foods are prepared with a careful consideration for implications on the body. As a firm activist of health awareness, Richard proclaims, "The feedback box is right by the till and we're always listening." As a cook and a certified "lover of food," Richard admits, "I had to make sure I was eating the right foods and dieting correctly. The body is a temple and you have to look after it!"

More than just a restaurant, since opening in the 1990s from just a single unit almost a third of the size of the premises today, Richard describes the opportunity to create a space that also served as an educational centre. With the walls donned with informative Afro-Caribbean memorabilia, Richard's extensive time spent researching and striving toward a certain level of ambience, plus peeking in the kitchen of any restaurant that he visits across the world has made Jamaican Ways the place it is today.

Don's Hut

Tooting, SW London

On a Friday night the vivacious atmosphere of Don's hut is reminiscent of long-running British TV show Eastenders' Queen Victoria pub. Those who have been absent for more than a few weeks are met with cheers as they share stories about their travels and mishaps. Regulars slowly file into the shop's space and by the time business begins to wind down at around 10pm everyone in shop has a cup in hand with "good-stuff" flowing.

This sense of community, owner-chef Cory Joseph suggests is down to the affinity of the long-standing team who are all familiar with many of the regular customers. The other reason why the shop may have come to exist as such a popular communal hub, some suggest may be a result of the increasing decline of social spaces owned and predominantly aimed at Caribbean commerce as regulars recount tales of places such as Oasis, Belaire and Rosemary's.

Don's Hut, originally opened in 2004 by Cory's father Don Joseph, was an instant hit in Southwest London's Tooting Broadway area as the local Caribbean populace instantly found a welcoming environment to congregate.

The business' roots stem back to the late 1970s when Don, after coming to Britain from Lindon, the second largest town in Guyana, became a known figure across London selling hard food produce such as yams, green banana and plantain in a number of notable markets such as Hammersmith and Brixton's market on Electric Avenue. This was a time when such produce was hard to source and not as widely available as it is now for the everyday customer.

Having soared to heights of popularity in this trade, Don was able to act on an opportunity that arose in the Tooting region of southwest London, catering to people in Streatham, Wandsworth and everywhere in between, plus many from further afield who were accomplices of Don in his early days of trading.

With the ethos of community at the core of the business, the shop grew from strength to strength, and when Don retired from the business it was a natural progression for his son Cory to take over after having more than two decades of classical culinary training under his belt. Cory sought to leave the classic Caribbean components of the shop's menu untouched and then implement key learnings from these distinct French and Italian cuisines that he had picked up over the years and embed them into the composition of the shop's existing Caribbean cuisine. "That's how we been so successful at appealing to a wider crowd," reflects Cory. Furthermore, being influenced by Asian food and a consideration for the nuances of different spices allowed Cory to experiment and find some new crowd pleasers such as their sweet chilli wings (pictured next page.)

Complimenting the daily cooked meals such as the saltfish, brown stew, jerk chicken and curry mutton meal is the shops jar of self made hot pepper sauce lying in an small unsuspecting ceramic pot on the counter. One of the regular characters in the shops exclaims "That's the hottest sauces inna inglan!" and for the novice spice consumer a cup of milk or the shops creamy Guinness punch, carrot juice or Irish moss is a must to combat the inevitable fire induced on the tongue. With the sauce now readily available for enticed customers to purchase, featuring official packaging being designed by Cory, this expedition gives heed to the expansion plans of the shop in the near future. Cory suggests, "Hopefully there will be some space to play Dominos!"

Tel: 020 8767 9

DON'S
CARRIBEAN

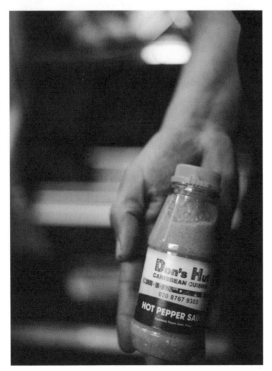

Coconut Kitchen
Islington, N London

Most evenings, after finishing the preparation for the select meals of the day, Everall Hall, known simply to scores of regulars as 'Chef,' can be found relaxing under the gaze of many of his own paintings, including an almost photographic oil reproduction of his original stomping ground, West Green Road in North London, and a portrait of Britain's first Black member of Parliament, Bernie Grant. However, it was not painting nor cooking that originally led 'Chef' to become a popular figure across the local London area and further afield.

Originally, cutting his teeth in the music industry as a record producer back home in August Town, Jamaica, with his own titled 'Eckeelous Movement Sound' he, alongside friends 'Bombshell' & Ashley K, recorded and collaborated with many world famous Dancehall music stars such as Sizzla, Eterna and Dwayne Stevenson before a move across the Atlantic was on the cards.

Chef recalls that his move away from the music world to the food world in the late 1980s was largely due to the ill-fated event of a marauding landlord changing the locks of his 'Dee-Vibes Studio' in Stoke Newington, North London with all the equipment still inside. This happened to coincide with the time when the area had began to become more upmarket.

Over the years, regardless of numerous counts of harassment from the local constabulary, the studio had become a pit stop for local MC's and Deejays to cut sounds, hone their lyrics and in general become a commune with nothing but the passion of music at its core. With that in mind, its no wonder that Chef can often be seen embracing the microphone and MC'ing when the music bug hits him throughout the week - though this is usually reserved for the functions held at the restaurant late on a Saturday night.

Chef's culinary journey since that time in the early 1990s took him all over North and East London, cooking at many long-gone, but highly regarded establishments such as Chef Again, Platinum Sweet in Lea Bridge Road, and the Plus One Club in Dalston. With this, dishes at Coconut Kitchen are a culmination of decades of these experiences plus the creative freedom of ownership.

All this has allowed for some rarities such as their fish tea, a leaner version of soup and 'sea-puss' punch, sea-puss being Jamaican slang for octopus, a catchphrase that was stamped in history by Little Audrey's "Sea Puss and Bammie" record for Studio One. Amongst a cluster of indispensable dishes cooked when occasion calls, the curried and stewed octopus provide the impetus of conversation between many of the locals who stop in even to just check up on Chef and his wife or to quickly check any sports results.

Ragga's
Liverpool

"The first day was crazy, we sold out everything. All the food was gone!" recalls Verdain Griffin, part of the family team behind Liverpool's Ragga's, which from upstart beginnings has grown into the city's largest collection of Caribbean food stops encompassing components of takeaway, cafés, bars and restaurants. "Back in the [19]80s, in frontline times all you could find was small shops with just seasoned chicken and dumplings. That was it," Verdain adds. With a vision to create something more inviting for the people of the northwest, Ragga's began trading in 2006.

"The name comes from Ragga himself, who was a local legend around here. He was from Jamaica and from way back he used to cook out of his house for people in the area." As the bio then adds, "Ragga was an island celebrity! His recipes were renowned for their ability to combine originality with his own signature twist and you know that he only believed in using the freshest ingredients." Following a stint in Jamaica, Verdain caught a cooking passion and ideas started to swell. "A while back I visited Negril, Falmouth and a few other places in Jamaica and my friends would always show me all the cooking basics."

Proposing the idea to Ragga that they should come together to start a more fitting establishment than his own home's kitchen, which had been a popular food pick-up spot the team acquired a small property from a friend that was located on Smithdown Road in Liverpool's Toxteth area, known to often locals as "L8" or Liverpool 8 due to the areas postcode, where for years they worked on building a consistent level of customer service and experimenting with a wide-ranging menu. Once opened the team ploughed ahead full steam before Ragga departed back to Jamaica.

To this day taking inspiration from Ragga's own original recipes from back home in Port Antonio in Portland, Verdain suggests, "Our style is home cooked food because often people want a hearty meal," whilst adding, "There is a compromise, however, you have to meet customers in the middle, with things like bones especially, as some of people have never had Caribbean food before." Taking stock not just from his own Caribbean heritage, Verdain describes how his Italian heritage plays just as much a role in the foundation of Ragga's. "My mum and her side of the family were always cooking Italian food at home and I remember always watching," he explains, illustrating an appreciation for the laid back yet sophisticated nature of his family's Italian cooking.

With this formula firmly in place, "As the restaurants grew so did our team, from mums to brothers to sisters, Ragga's turned in to a family affair." Growing from the Toxteth outpost to a café restaurant on Liverpool's bohemian Lark Lane before opening up their largest offering on Bold Street, often mentioned alongside the likes of London's Brick Lane or Manchester's Canal Street. After the family grew with a team of Griffins youngers, the brothers' decided to focus just on the single original Toxteth site. "It's harder to maintain your standard once you start expanding with a chain so we try and keep things simple" Verdain details.

Keeping it simple is exactly what Raggas does and as such can ensure quality in all their meals be it the jerk chicken, oxtail or curry mutton. Additionally, the shop takes advantage of Liverpool's coastal proximity with the likes of their jerk prawns and boneless tilapia. Although Liverpool's Canada docks are some way off from the golden sands of Jamaica, the Ragga's family endeavour to bring some island sunshine to England's northwest.

One Stop
Harlesden, NW London

Sharing its name with Reggae artist Derrick Hariott's legendary One Stop Record shop in Jamaica's capital city Kingston, One Stop Restaurant founded in 1998 was a relatively new addition to the Caribbean landscape between north west London's Harlesden High Street and Craven Park Road. However, now approaching two decades in business the restaurant has grown to achieve high levels of prominence beyond the streets of NW10 from everywhere between Harrow and Northwest London down across the River Thames to Southwest London. Popularity boomed so much for the shop's delivery service that they had to restrict the number of postcodes they delivered to after the hungry mouths in forty plus postcodes proved somewhat of a stretch for the kitchen crew along with the streams of local customers eating in.

Whilst most of the earlier Caribbean food businesses in the direct area focused on providing takeaway services befitting the space available to them, Veanna Dixon's One Stop filled a much needed service in the area offering an eat in dining service from 9am all the way up until 11pm. Given the change in Harlesden's ethnic makeup in the early 2000s, the restaurant aimed not just to be a hub for the local Caribbean community but a place to engage and educate newly landed peoples from South America to Eastern European about the joys of the Caribbean and its cuisine.

The walls are lined with classic photographic imagery of Jamaica food such as ackee and breadfruit taken by renowned Jamaican photographer Ray Chen and paintings by Trinidadian artist Angus Bascombe, which although the names may not ring bells for many the images resonate deep nostalgia to the homes of older family members growing in the Caribbean and decades gone by in the UK.

During the Commonwealth and Olympic games, above the heads of passing customers, string banners containing flags of the world from the Caribbean, to Africa, India and the Americas decorated the shop. This in a sense represented the cosmopolitan feel that Noz, Sophie (pictured) and family have created at One Stop, which in many ways has become a one-stop shop for the local community. Bringing in chefs deriving from not just the Caribbean but from Italy to China, the family hopes this sense of multiculturalism will assist in a level of diversity that along with a shop expansion will continue One Stop's ascension for another two decades.

The restaurant's all encompassing Caribbean menu extends to the likes of fresh Trinidadian style dhalpouri roti and people from all walks come in not only to feast on the array of quick dishes such as patties, festivals and fried dumplings but plates of more hearty meals such as the mutton and chicken meals. These come in boneless versions to entice those who didn't grow up with the meals and aren't used to the sight and sounds of dispensing bones common to a homely Caribbean dinner table.

For those not fortunate enough to be brisk walk away from Harlesden's High Street, the family has created their own iPhone and Android app to entice customers throughout the week.

With the sounds of the Stone Love sound system nestled in the corner of the restaurant carrying on the tradition of marketing the latest sounds from the islands direct to expatriates and aficionados, often you find many just visit the shop as a means of escapism from the hustle and bustle of London to cast their minds back to a sunnier place if just for a moment.

Rum Shack

Pollokshaws, Glasgow

On a road with split loyalties between local fierce football rivals of Glasgow Rangers and Celtic FC those of all walks of life find middle ground at Rum Shack. The restaurant founded in 2014 by Tobago born Brian Austin and tight-knit crew has been a breath of fresh tropical air in the southside of the Scottish town in a country that has a dearth of options when it comes to Caribbean food.

Brian tells of how hard it was to find Caribbean food back in the days when he first arrived in Scotland. "I was hungry for some curry goat, stew chicken, macaroni pie and pilau. I moved here in 1992 from Trinidad and Tobago. I missed the food from home and always wanted there to be a place in Glasgow that served up those dishes. I didn't think I would be the one to do it. Whenever I imagined it, I was always the happy customer."

After some years when that magical mirage of Caribbean food still never appeared, Brian, enterprise partner Lewis Macaulay and crew set about changing this. Starting out on the street food and events scene, Brian recalls, "we were invited to do a few local things in Glasgow. I think the first thing was a Lee Scratch Perry gig. We did a few street food showdowns that helped raise our profile and then we managed to keep it going. I think the furthest North we went was Inverness."

Since the Brian says that reception from the Scottish audience has been very supportive, though he tells a humorous story, "I remember we did something up in Perth and a lady couldn't accept that we were selling goat. I never figured out exactly why. I remember she was not happy though! Can't please everyone!" While nobody might think of similarities between Trinidad and Scotland, the two nations some 4,300 miles away share a host of food fixations.

The student staple of cheesy fries is given a Caribbean makeover here doused with jerk seasoning and melted cheese then covered with jerk pork gravy. Additionally, the Chicken Brown Down dish consisting of a sumptuous stew chicken served up with a Macaroni pie that has long been an island favourite and recently made its way into Scottish lore when Scottish head, Nicola Sturgeon announced herself as an advocate for the snack. Both regions are crusaders for all things battered and fried. With this, their jerk fish and chips (pictured opposite) has proved to be a real winner simultaneously appealing to Caribbean food aficionados and local Scots alike.

The deftest of feats for the Rum Shack came when they invited the Belmont Royal Scotsman esteemed chef Mark Tamburrini into the fold. This led to the inventive creation of their spiced haggis bon bons (pictured next page.) Here, the legendary Scottish foodstuff of haggis meat is rolled in bread crumbs, deep-fried, and served up with a tangy tamarind sauce. The less brave opt for an equally tasty vegan version or a host of other Tobagan favourites like doubles and tostones, fritters made from boiled plantain, whizzed up with allspice, ground coriander, and coconut milk.

While Scotland doesn't have the largest Caribbean diaspora, the nation's history with the tropical region stems back centuries to the 18th century when the transatlantic slave trade was underway. This brought many Scots to the region, some voluntary and some forced. The legacy of this today is seen in rum commerce and The Rum Shack pay homage to this evidently in their name and also the one hundred strong list of rums. In order to provide patrons something different, the outfit always has a "break even rum" on the go. These are so exclusive the only joy they seek in selling it is to bring joy rather than any form of profit. At this time, said rum is a sleek 1992 bottle of Hampden Estate, a company that provides a fitting case study into Scotland's existence in the Caribbean.

Directly next door to the restaurant Is the Dancehall, a space fostered by the crew in order to help provide an alternative groove for the local residents and beyond. Here, they host a continual stream of live shows and bookings with local talent as well as Caribbean music icons. Even old Scottish traditions like Burns Night are embraced and remixed with a reggae twist. Be it food or music, the crew here are passionate about sustaining Caribbean culture in this corner of the world.

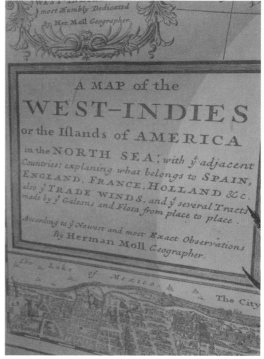

Mullins Brasserie

Margate, Kent

Though for decades there has been a sizeable Caribbean presence in Kent, the south-eastern region of the UK, opportunities for Caribbean food are far and few between in the area. Even with this, Mullins' Brasserie aims to not be pigeonholed and impress for any genre. The Brasserie, located in the coastal seaside town of Margate was the long-time vision of Antonio (Tony) Forde that finally came to fruition in 2010 after he hopped back and forth between the town and his home in Barbados for a number of years.

Mullins Brasserie is housed in a converted old butchers' shop and former brasserie, where Tony himself one previously worked. He explains that the opportunity came to take over the old English public house style and he and his wife Marianne jumped at it. The building is nestled in the heart of the Old Town that is packed with similar classical architecture. This perfectly fits the goal of the outfit to offer a warm and inviting ambiance that combines many of the building's original features accompanied with contemporary furnishings striving toward the end result of a comfortable, relaxed and intimate dining experience.

Tony's past endeavours manning the kitchens at several of Barbados' top hotels and restaurants. With this, the restaurant pays homage to Mullins beach located in the parish of St. Peters to the Northwest of the island and Tony has looked to incorporate elements of Caribbean flavours and techniques into his cooking. The end result is a selection of innovative dishes infrequently seen elsewhere that are elegantly presented and most importantly to Tony "very tasty!!"

While the beachfront of Margate isn't exactly the sunny shores of Barbados, the region of Kent and Margate in addition to nearby towns like Deal and Whitstable have their own vibrant seafood ecosystem and fresh produce that Mullins take full advantage of. Here, Mullins' menu comprises modern a vivid mix of European cuisine with a generous dash of Caribbean flavour. For the starters, the salt and pimento spiced battered calamari is a winner as evidenced by the amount of times you'll see it trotted out to the customers out front basking in the sun and the ackee and salted codfish lightly cooked in coconut milk is an inviting way of introducing the people of the area to this island favourite. The early star here though, and a personal favourite of Tony himself are the Bajan fishcakes, a popular snack back home that Tony has refined, served with a creamy yet tantalising scotch bonnet pepper mayonnaise.

The mains also do well to shine a light on the region's vast array of pescatarian specialties with creole fish stew, red stripe beer battered fish goujons and a pan-fried blackened swordfish that is served with naturally honeyed roasted sweet potatoes, corn on the cob and escovitch dressing.

Beyond this, local farms supply a variety of produce that goes into the other eye-pleasing plates. Vegans are satiated with the coconut rooted Ital Rastafarian stew and creole vegetables served with grilled tofu and halloumi. The ravished carnivores are of course in for a treat. The jerk process isn't just reserved for chicken but also sausages plated up with penne pasta, mushrooms and a creamy jerk cheddar sauce. Moreover, the extensive drink collection that does well to highlight Bajan beverages are also utilised in the kitchen with a traditional favourite of oxtail prepared by a braising process in Guinness & red wine.

While the nearby beachfront is lined with old shops selling countless amounts of traditional British seaside confectionary, here you will find a more sophisticated roster of sweets permeated with Caribbean energy. Be it the ginger sponge with toffee sauce and vanilla ice cream, the rich brownies or mango and white chocolate cheesecake. Tony states that his ambition here was to present Caribbean food in a sophisticated way and finishing off the meal with the Caribbean darling rum and raisin bread and butter pudding paired with lightly spiced custard is a testimony to this.

RiveRLife
Haymarket, Edinburgh

Opportunities for authentic French Caribbean food anywhere on the British Isles are extremely rare. With this, for a country like Scotland with scant Caribbean eating options the presence of RiveRLife, a Guadeloupe inspired outfit has been a slow burning revelation. Opened in 2012, the restaurant's lively aura and tropical vibration proved a welcome aide to the sporadic sun spells of the locale and helped locals jet thousands of miles away if just for the hours spent eating inside.

The restaurant is the combination of the enterprising know-how of Zambian born Buumba Stacy Mweetwa and culinary expertise of husband Mario Leon Caneval who hails from Marie-galante of Guadeloupe and came to the UK in 1995. That same aforementioned scarcity of Caribbean food in Edinburgh and Scotland in general was the impetus for opening the restaurant Buumba explains. However, existing in this Bermuda triangle of the food world had its pros and cons in the early days.

"Initially, we can say, people were unsure about our food" However, early interest was buoyed by the fact that locals and tourists alike had tried either French or Caribbean or both cuisines before. Buumba adds, "numbers were rising slightly but surely. It was a very slow and difficult start. It seems like it was an overnight turn around when we can say the response became overwhelmingly positive, I guess that's why riveRLife Restaurant is still in business eight years after opening its doors."

It seems in general that the overall positive attitude in, and interest to once unfamiliar foods has developed and this has had a spillover benefit here. The hardest part is getting people inside and to the dining tables and the food takes care of the rest. Buumba details, "the traditional word of mouth referrals have all led to more customers coming in," potentially based on her "au naturale people personality" at front of house. She continues, "over the years, we have heard from more and more customers saying, once they tried our food, they cannot resist coming back for more. The more adventurous customers, have worked their way through the menu and keep going round in circles, whilst others have picked their favourite dishes and stick to them,

some will just not see beyond one dish."

The menu is an exemplary display of Guadeloupean heritage that pays homage as much as it does to the lauded traditions of French food as it does to the creolisation of eating synonymous with the Caribbean. In an area as cosmopolitan as Edinburgh many are already familiar with the likes of pork liver parfait, fricassee and blue cheese stuffed mushrooms. Mario perfected these dishes across a tenured career that included a stay in France some years ago. This notability gets people in the door who are then introduced to a world of island favourites like saltfish accra consisting of bitesize fritters served with homemade sauce chien Provençal salsa and mainstay jerk chicken playfully thrown into a salad.

Amongst the pillars of the menu here however is the colombo, the famed curry dish (pictured next page) of Martinique, Guadeloupe and a host of other islands. Colombo is a creole curry transported to the previously mentioned islands by indentured laborers from India and Sri Lanka. These were individuals who worked the sugar plantations of the French and other European colonists in the 19th and 20th century. The colombo is a mixture of various spices like turmeric, allspice and cumin that are as familiar now in the Caribbean as they are on the Indian subcontinent. This concoction is slowly heated and readied for the addition of chicken, fish or the chickpea option and cooked in a typical unhurried Caribbean fashion for maximum flavour infusion.

It seems whenever and however people have an interaction with Guadeloupe they are hooked be it holidays or honeymoons. Buumba jests that even the TV series Death in Paradise, which is filmed in Guadeloupe, seems to have also played a part in getting people through the door. Mario expresses, "home is home and will always be home" adding, "I miss cultivating, fishing and eating more organic food. I miss the more stable weather, the outdoor spaces. I miss going to the beach without having to worry that the weather may change to the other extreme." While Mario isn't able to get back to Guadeloupe as often as he'd like these days, it seems replicating its food and seeing customers' jubilant responses to his home food provides a type of catharsis.

Fish, Wings & Tings

Brixton Village, SW London

Whilst a relatively new addition to the Brixton food scene, Fish, Wings & Ting was many years in making. "I had the idea in my head many many years ago as young man and I always knew it would work!" exclaims chef and owner Brain Danclair. What wasn't a part of that vision however was the exact location of that foresight. As a frequent visitor to the local Brixton market and some of the area's older Caribbean food spots, a chance walk through The Granville Arcade (now known as Brixton Village) meant that the location chose Brian rather than vice versa. "The office down there was open, I went in to ask about any potential spaces and not a week later I was here!"

Already an established name as a chef in the USA and UK, the restaurant is not only a product of Brian's illustrious career in the kitchen as much as it is attributable to a youth spent eagerly cooking beside elder family members back home in the Port of Spain, Trinidad. Here, his family, especially his grandmother were famed cooks across the whole community. "People from all over would always come round to have some of our food" Brian recalls and the atmosphere of Fish, Wings and Ting perhaps is more a reflection of that friendly, laid back vibe than that with which Brian would go on to cut his culinary teeth.

Moving to the United States for school, Brian ended up taking a shine to high-end culinary cooking and when a stint under the wing of famed chef Yannick Cam at his renowned restaurant Provence fared very well there was no turning back. "Provence was very high end French cuisine and so I definitely learned a lot about the whole business there."

With the foundation he obtained there, after a move across the Atlantic to London in 2001, Brian continued on his thread of working in the fine dining scene. Working at five-star hotels and high-end establishments in London where he was head chef, this was a continuation of his bistro influence résumé, focused on the continental benchmarks of coq au vin, risotto, pancetta and the likes accompanied by crystalline glasses of aged wine.

Given all this, when the time came to branch off and do something of his own, Caribbean food was at the forefront of his mind. Speaking on his early interaction with the landscape Brian remarks, "I wasn't entirely happy with what I saw when I came over to London and I thought I could do something quite different and unique."

Whilst Trinidadian delicacies still lie somewhat on the fringes of the mainstream Caribbean menu, Brian was of the opinion he could also help further change the perception of his home island food, "Beyond just the typical Indo-Trinidadian cuisine that people know," he demonstrates. "There are so many regions and so much more to explore. The creole element of the cuisine has been marginalised. Its not just roti, there's other things like trini callaloo, curried crabs and pilau."

Fusing his professional experiences with a familiar homely vibe where bold colours reigned supreme, the shop's take on well regarded Caribbean dishes like curry goat and jerk chicken are immediately set apart from the rest. Brian's proclivity for taste and colour features heavily in the form of the signature rainbow dressings of purple coleslaw and glittering pineapple & mango chutney that instantly catch the eyes of passers-by. Once tempted in, the coconut curry prawns and Red Stripe battered tempura prawns prove seductive. As Brian gestures, even the menu's "Small Tings" he wanted to be different. "We have things like the tamarind sauce and ginger and lime aioli, which really adds to the dishes."

After service has wound down, the scores of pleased customers who are sprawled out on the Arcade's foyer relax and let the roti settle in with a pitcher of rum. If the restaurant's sound system cable ends up with Brian, more often than not you can be assured the frenetic, rhythmic sound of Soca is about to hit the airwaves.

Rhythm Kitchen

London

For Delroy Dixon, Caribbean food and culture is a way of life not just eating. It's community, its togetherness and most importantly it's fun. This passion was so fierce that it was only a matter of time before he would set up his own outlet for it and as such, Rhythm Kitchen was born in 2010. As a TV producer, Delroy was always a creative at the core though after many years, eventually that industry could not provide the cultural avenues for gratification that he needed. With a strong Jamaican food heritage passed down from his parents, the call for a physical station to embody this became overwhelming.

Delroy describes the origins of Rhythm Kitchen explaining, "it came about because we used to do these big family barbecues and we thought it would be a great idea to open a restaurant." Around this time a new shopping centre was being built in East London not far from the area Delroy grew up in and knowing the cultural make-up of the place it seemed like a perfect for. Though he had never run a full-fledged restaurant before, such was the passion of his application and the demonstration of local knowledge that they were granted the location and Rhythm Kitchen grew from there.

With the shopping centre in close proximity to the London Olympics site that hosted the international games in 2012 Rhythm Kitchen became of a hub for celebration of the team's success and culture in general and this merriment is something Delroy has always looked to cultivate. For this to truly bloom Delroy explains, "we knew that to grow the business we really had to be on the high street. We heard about Jerk Hut on Hoe Street in Walthamstow going up for sale and we knew it had traded well there." They went into talks and eventually Rhythm Kitchen in Walthamstow in 2018.

From an early age, Delroy explains how he wanted to be a chef and through different stints in and out of the industry this lifelong yearning has reared itself in the vibrant menu at Rhythm Kitchen. Here Delroy wanted to not only commemorate his Jamaican upbringing but also the wider Caribbean community. The jerk options of pork and chicken have been winners from day one. The meats are left to marinate for 24 hours in a family concoction of herbs and spices before being finished on the grill then caressed with the gravy of the same marinade. All are served with options of white rice, rice and peas and even Trinidadian roti flatbread sourced from the nearby powerhouse of Horizon foods. (p.70)

This jerk process lends itself well to the pescatarian parts of the menu that include an extremely generous whole select fish as well as grilled salmon and coconut peppered prawns.

Other specialties cooked up by Delroy and crew include a sumptuous slow-cooked braised oxtail in a rich sauce with butter beans among others that are all bolstered by a tempting list of sides such as satlfish or plantain fritters and sweet fried dumplings. These same techniques and flavours are also equally on show in the vegan dishes like the savoury Trinidadian channa chickpea and potato curry as well the Rastafari-Jamaican inspired Ragga stew constructed with red kidney beans and packed starchy yams and handmade boiled dumplings.

Utilising the seemingly endless array of incredible rum that descends from the Caribbean islands, Delroy started a Monday night rum that in order to raise the profile of certain favourites but also to foster a local community around Caribbean culture that ended up bringing together people from all corners of the UK. This sense of commune is something that Delroy is keen to continue into the future and situates Rhythm Kitchen as more than a place to just come and eat or takeaway.

Ayanna's
Canary Wharf, E London

Under the skyline of East London's Dockland's district, the glow from Canary Wharf illuminates golden parquet flooring and rows of immaculate white tables topped with an assortment of minimalist design inspired servings. Originally opened in 2012, the Fisher family at Ayanna's London now carries the baton passed on from the inventiveness of acclaimed Jamaican chef Collin Brown, who laid the establishment's foundations.

Christened after youngest in-house family member and kitchen prodigy Ayanna, the name means beautiful flower in the Swahili language. Here, that nature of elegance is applied to an à la carte of Caribbean classics like brown stew chicken, curry goat and oxtail, with the addition of many signature twists and dazzling visuals. With one of Chef Brown's understudies staying on, combined with the Fisher parents having years of experience under their belt working for Port Royal Patties, the polished and cultivated but characteristically Caribbean nature of the menu remained integral.

While items such as the spicy whitebait fish and duck breast or callaloo pancake rolls may sound removed from what might be expected at a distinctively Caribbean restaurant, eldest daughter Aisha Fisher recalls, "From the beginning it was always important for us to support local and independent business, especially people where we are from.

All our meat is from Malcolm's Butchers in Willesden (Northwest London), on special occasions like Mothers' Day and Valentines' Day we have a florist who decorates the whole restaurant with floral bouquets." Additionally, on weekends when the smooth sounds of Lovers Rock are given a rest, she elaborates, "We have a live Piano player and singer to add to the mood."

Sticking to the fundamentals of their Caribbean upbringing was key to the restaurant flourishing. "It was tough in the beginning - really tough. It was the peak of the recession and there were many sleepless nights!" However, tough grit from the entire family who all in some capacity help out at the restaurant and the friendly charm of professional barman Conner all helped out.

Rounding off a list of tropical deserts, including mango sorbet and home-made banana cake, the implementation of their signature red label rum cake proved such a hit that the family is now expanding the offerings with their Ayannas Bakery brand, extending their rum based recipes to a number of other baked goods.

"We felt there wasn't anywhere in London that served our food in this type of environment, especially around here," Aisha describes, though happily telling, "Mum was such a good cook, we didn't have a great need to go out to find Caribbean food that much, and living in our area of London it wasn't hard to get the ingredients with all the local shops."

With the family having moved to London from Trelawney Parish, Cornwall County in the early 2000s, this experience is a stark contrast to those who came decades before and their modern viewpoint and approach is observable throughout the restaurant.

With the family passionate about bringing a fragment of their homeland to London, amongst plans to use the restaurant walls as forums for Jamaican culture and artists, they even made the decision to forego various easier to obtain coffee brands and directly source Jamaica's Blue Mountain Coffee. As Aisha reminisces, "There's just a smell you only get with Blue Mountain." With all these senses covered, Aisha proclaims, "The only thing missing is the sun and the breeze!"

Rudie's

London

Rudie's restaurant is the brainchild of years of planning that in 2015 found north east London's Dalston and Stoke Newington area to be the perfect location for their first take on Caribbean food in a welcoming local environment before branching out down the road in Shoreditch and then beyond. The flair of Rudie's menu pays homage to Jamaica's rich and diverse composition originating from east Asian spices to the fruit and vegetation of west Africa in much the same way that all the differing locations of Rudie's does. In this melting pot, Rudie's have worked to create the perfect platform that could exist between the rich Afro-Caribbean heritage of London, the UK, and the growing influx of eager diners from across the world.

The outfit draws on co-founder Michelle's Jamaican family upbringing, extensive travel research and of course eating on the island. It's no wonder then that the food at Rudie's is described as "unmistakably" Jamaican. Given this grounding and heritage, it was impossible for the pair to cut certain corners when it came to the main facets of the restaurant's dining experience. This is notable in the likes of their jerk meals where the meat is marinated, at minimum for 24 hours and naturally, (as most jerk connoisseurs will tell you,) can only be considered "real" jerk if it has been cooked in a traditional steel drum. These drums are a common sight at all of their locations be it their numerous street food pop-ups or restaurants.

Wherever Rudie's operate they take on the role of ambassadors of Caribbean culture with glee livening up their surroundings with the bubbling sounds of Reggae and Dancehall. Their original line-up of goings-on throughout the week included "Jerk Monday's" serving to cure Monday blues with half price jerk chicken, and Wednesday's "Bun N Beer" offering of a icy glass of Red Stripe, fries and choice of jerk cheese burger, jerk pork or the swordfish/crispy calamari. All these not only keep fans well fed but provided a fun entry point for many into the regions' vivid food.

As anyone who has first-hand experience of visiting the Caribbean or attending a Caribbean function can attest, the drinks are just as important as food and Rudie's has placed as much extensive care in their drink selection as the food and dining experience. This is seen instantly with their selection of carefully curated drinks bolstered by a partnership with the world-famous Appleton Estate Jamaica Rum and additionally featuring the likes of Blackwell, Monymusk and Edwin Charley Proprietor's Collection. Paired with a team of dazzling mixologists, the well-named cocktail offerings provide an entertaining talking point with their diverse nods to Caribbean history.

These feature the "AD1494", "The Colony", "Ole Money" and the "Selassie I." The "Dr No," features a suave Portobello Gin cucumber Martini, referencing the first James Bond film and the "Jamaica Nice" includes a "typical blend of all things nice, epitomising Jamaican beach life," featuring a fruity boozy smoothie with almond syrup, lime, nectarine, pineapple, Appleton and coconut rum. Convincingly, this eccentric mix of flavours and colours fully embodies the aura that Rudie's has created.

Pull Up Bar Cafe
Manchester

When The Drop hit Manchester's suburban region of Chorlton in 2015, the restaurant's rum bar accompanied with its modern take on Caribbean food proved an instant hit around a quaint but thriving area described by locals as a "city within a city." After the founders parted ways, co-founder Ez continued his flair and passion for Caribbean food at his Pull Up Bar Cafe. Ez, (who comes from a lineage of Caribbean lore in Manchester – his father Aval is behind the city's Kool Runnings chain p.149) along with a crew of family and friends have endeavoured to create a vibrant and lively space with an emphasis on good food, good music and a focus on quality.

With food sourced locally from farmhouses and markets across the northwest of England, the crew looked for a unique take on traditional Caribbean dishes that have been inspired from a life growing up working with, and eating foods from the islands supplemented by several excursions there. Here, the crew have encapsulated the famed laid-back beauty of the Caribbean with their multi-coloured wooden decor they instantaneously transports those inside to more tropical pastures.

The food here of course does the same. With the jerk chicken for example, the crew describes, "we barbeque-smoke our chicken the traditional way, with hickory, pimento wood chips or pimento corns depending on what we can get our hands on," and with the curry goat, "It's all in the long marinade. We've left the classic flavours there and finished with mango yogurt, pomegranate and coriander." The cafe is heavily inspired by the mixed heritage of the Caribbean and this constantly weaves its way through the menu from the big plates and mains. The Cafe does well to show the full versatility of Caribbean food techniques ensuring that novices and enthusiasts alike can all find favourites in the food.

The jerk halloumi and flavoursome feta and hummus salad are great takes on the middle eastern favourites. More so, chilli and ginger marinated lamb chops and the seasoned Caribbean steak and chips give new life to the northern British classic. The cafe even transforms the usually savoury served fried festival dumpling into a sweet dessert filled with hot chocolate sauce and paired with milk chocolate and rum sauce. All plates are designed for sharing so whatever is chosen, eventually everyone can work their way towards finding a favourite.

Later on in the week on Sundays, in the midst of a flowing exotic cocktail menu, the "Reggae Roast" and the gluten free "Rasta Roast" provide a perfect example of the restaurant's multicultural fusion of flavours. This picturesque dish includes roast butternut squash or pumpkin plus a pepper, spring onions and olive mix (and feta cheese for "part-time rastas") accompanying roast carrot, sweet potato, and the usual suspects of fried plantain, rice 'n' peas and gravy. All this has led to some of the most eye-pleasing dishes in the whole city. If there's any space left for dessert the Ballin' banana fritters do just the trick.

Spiced Roots

Cowley Road, Oxford

Ever since Jammo first came to England in 1998 from Port of Spain, the capital of Trinidad and Tobago he immersed himself in British food culture. Adventuring into the highbrow world of fine dining as he tells, "I liked the presentation but the atmosphere or flavour". With Caribbean food evidently part of his DNA he wanted to find food he liked and envisaged a space complete with professional service but also a relaxed Caribbean vibe, "the best of both worlds" he adds.

Enter Spiced Roots, opened to the people of Oxford and beyond in 2016. Jammo forwards, "how people see Italian, Indian, Chinese food for example… I wanted to enter that realm." Spiced Roots mission to alter this perception is double-sided according to Jammo from within the Caribbean community and outside. "We devalue our own food" he posits. The admittedly cheap price of island food often prevents some from supporting restaurants and balking at the comparatively expensive prices. "Look at gnocchi for example, it's the same flour and same water we use but people look down at our food."

This esteem or lack thereof toward Caribbean food in Jammo's opinion doesn't match the technique and quality of his and the wider Caribbean communities' food. He posits, "a French restaurant can command £100 per meal yet for our slow cooking food, real Michelin style stuff we receive nothing in comparison." For the 24 hour marinated meats and four-hour smoked and grilled chicken in a self-designed drum Spiced Roots believes their food matches anywhere let alone just the pigeonhole of Caribbean restaurants.

The tagline of spiced roots is *"a representation of the best the Caribbean region has to offer"* adding, "We take our craft extremely seriously and aim to create an unparalleled Caribbean gastronomical experience." Beyond re-imagining Caribbean food, he also hopes to widen the scope of how we understand the region's food beyond its modern imagery. The hieroglyphs on the wall point to a time before colonialism, Jammo explains, "to remind us that our history didn't start there." Jerk Chicken isn't big in Trinidad now he

details, but if you look at the Amerindian and Arawak tribal presence on the islands who preserved jerk in allspice seasoning for days, you'll see a long tradition of the mainstay that's now firmly owned by Jamaica.

The corn-fed jerk chicken experience at Spiced Roots is unlike anywhere else in the UK, artfully placed on slate plates amid a pan-African dance of red, gold and green sweet bells peppers before paint brush strokes of puree finish the dish. Here, Beetroot mash, mango and smooth peas are used to match the aforementioned colour scheme.

The rest of the menu is constantly evolving to incorporate the freshest local seasonal produce representing the breadth and diversity of the Caribbean. Jamaican favourites like oxtail swimming in soft boiled butter beans and whole roasted snapper are on offer. Jetting off to the other side of Caribbean, the beef centred Guyanese Pepper Pot accompanied with cornmeal dumplings has proved a hit with the locals with its sweet base as has the tamarind glazed rump of lamb inspired by the same easterly region.

With representation of the restaurant rooted in Trinidad and Tobago, it goes without saying that the islands along with their Indian heritage would infiltrate the menu. Fried vegetables snacks like saheena and spinach bhaji are nods to street food icons however the ultimate indicator of this is the roti. The Rastafari vegan culture provides as much meat-free inspiration as the Indian heritage does and foods like the coconut and pumpkin rundown and the ackee with slow roasted tomatoes with Jerk Tempeh can all be happily served with the roti too.

It is likely you didn't even have to make it this far to be awed by Spiced Roots. The rum bar, with its long list of high-volume percentage beverages are again inspired by all corners of the Caribbean and are alchemised into an endless variety of cocktails. For the ultimate night of island culture, stay at Spiced Roots until final doors and then hop a just a few steps up Cowley Road to the legendary Hi-Lo Jamaican bar (p.230) for some smooth dub sounds and drinks into the early hours.

Three Little Birds

London

April Jackson has long been on a mission to change the image the world has of the country she was raised in and loves – Jamaica. The current outlet of this undertaking is the pioneering Three Little Birds series of Restaurants in South London and the activism associated with its existence.

As April tells, the inspiration behind the restaurant "was born out of the desire to combine my passion for food and Jamaica in order to create a career for myself whilst showcasing a different side of my country." Talking of the worldly negative perception Jamaica has, she tells that the country "is often perceived as either a ghetto or a beach; restaurants have to feature corrugated iron and decor that might be described as rustic but never luxurious." With Three Little Birds she is able to transcend clichés and challenge negative stereotypes with a high level of service accompanied with flavourful meals plated with finesse all combined in an atmosphere that is reminiscent of her Jamaican childhood.

Throughout her global travels, April has always held onto her Jamaican roots and flown the black, gold and green flag at the highest of peaks on various international platforms. Opened in 2015, Three Little Birds is a reflection and testimony of this. At the restaurant, reinterpreted classic Jamaican recipes are served up as sharing plates reminiscent of a summer's day in Catalonia. These are paired with cocktails based on the exceptional array of artisanal rum cocktails the Caribbean has to offer that line the walls of their outfits. April and company strive to do all this with a warm service that aims to breathe new life into Caribbean eateries as we may know them.

April's menu changes with the seasons every three months reflecting the timely produce available and allows for a level of flexibility that contributes to her vivid experiments. Halloumi fries and jerk seasoned hummus to nibble on for example, makes for a great introduction to this culinary exploration of Aprils'. For a slightly larger nibble that same hummus comes topped with a gleaming red tamarind sauce and then is adorned with a sizable jerk seasoned cauliflower. Be it the codfish fritters, jerk chicken, which here comes in burger form and honey glazed wings or the more traditional curry goat the restaurant endeavours to put their own refined spin on these dishes. On a number of nights per week, April, a self-taught business trailblazer and chef, can often be found heading the kitchen herself plating up these wonderful creations herself. If you can't make it to the restaurant, she chronicles many of these inventions on her blogs.

At the Brixton outpost, April's matches her acumen with the same passion for all things Jamaica. Here she frequently allocates space for all manner of island-inspired wares selling clothes, home-made snacks, books and more. Three Little Birds, sharing its name with the famous Bob Marley song are unashamedly champions for Jamaica and Jamaican culture. April's enterprising prowess was on full display to the people of the UK with her tenure on the renowned business reality TV show The Apprentice and that same prowess is on full display at Three Little Birds.

Buster Mantis

Deptford, SE London

Underneath the train tracks of Southeast London's Deptford Railway Station, a few steps from the home of Deptford's High Street Market, Buster Mantis is accommodated in a row of railway arches. A pair of arches encompasses a bar-restaurant and a creative space by day that by sunset is often transformed into a pulsating sweat-inducing dancefloor.

The name itself comes from the first Prime Minister of Jamaica, Sir Alexander Bustermante, the man enshrined on the $1 bill who played a key role in the movement for the independence of Jamaica, the country where the family behind Buster Mantis hails from. Manned primarily by Gordon McCowen, Buster Mantis has quickly cemented itself as a vibrant multifaceted space created on the lynchpin of a Caribbean, and notably Jamaican upbringing.

"That's what we know," Gordon remarks, "I grew up in Jamaica. The food we have is the food from home, the food that mum and gran would cook. Our family also had another Caribbean food place near here in New Cross some years ago." The tangy jerk chicken served up with rice n peas also finds its way into a lofty burger with avocado & coleslaw, whilst those with an aversion to meat can find solace in the chickpea, potato and pumpkin curry.

The restaurant places an emphasis on sourcing the majority of its ingredients locally to help keep the menu different, however there is a safe assurance that you will always be able to get the classics, such as ackee n' saltfish and curry.

"Authenticity is important to here," Gordon adds, regarding his home islands food. "Many people have never tried Jamaican food so we wanted the menu to reflect it, however we also wanted it so people who have never tried the food can get equally involved." Infusing the menu with dishes such as the pan-fried spicy filet of salmon is testament to this with its gloss of sweet potato mash. As is the small but highly moreish small plates of saltfish fritters, mackerel paté and avocado salsa accompanied by vibrant green plantain crisps.

Wanting to create a place in the area that was engaging to all facets of the local community, Gordon says, "We wanted to create this menu, but also we wanted to maintain it being very affordable. There's only one thing slightly above a tenner here!"

This community-facing viewpoint is then magnified with the Bar's adjacent creative space in "Arch 4" that now has hosted a swathe of exhibitions, film screenings, music shows, workshops and pop-ups from students and professionals alike. The space almost lent itself to it eludes Gordon. The aim was to give the occasional platform to creative and talented local people who don't always have the means or connections to access a similar kind of space.

Hand-built almost entirely by Gordon, family and friends, the tall willowy plants and the reclaimed wood hosting the backdrop of the Great bar (accommodating Brockley Brewery, Peckham Pils and understandably Red Stripe) and sturdy tables were crafted as a subtle nod to the family's recollection of their home in Mandeville, Jamaica. Replicating this laidback atmosphere in South London, Gordon suggests ultimately they just wanted to create somewhere local to hang out. Between the well stocked bar, innovative menu and calendar exhibitions there always seems a reason to.

BUSTER MANTIS

Ireland

If you've ever wondered why the famed Irish drink Guinness is so popular in the Caribbean community there is a deep history. The Irish presence in the Caribbean goes back centuries and ever since has inextricably linked the two regions some 4000 miles apart from each other. In Jamaica alone you'll find Irish Town and Dublin Castle in St. Andrew parish, Clonmel and Kildare in the parish of St. Mary, and Belfast and Middleton in that of St. Thomas. Throughout the Caribbean from Jamaica to Montserrat surnames such as Collins, Murphy, Madden, Mulling, McCarthy and McDonnough are all present too.

In the 17th century Irish dissidents to the powers in England were deported as indentured laborers to the Caribbean islands to work on sugar plantations. With the loss of land and financial resources incurred to many Irish, a great number flocked to the Caribbean as bonded contracted labourers. While many suffered at the hands of Protestant plantation owners' things here eventually got somewhat better for the Irish after their contracts ceased. Research suggests however, that as the African slave population grew and as the Irish's labour terms had been satisfied, the white Irish populace were able to move into better positions of power and political influence. This was also aided in participating in the military defence of the islands against other colonial powers. After this, a select few also went on to become merchants, traders and planters in the own right.

With the Irish remaining as an outcast community in England, the influx of Caribbean people to England after the World Wars once again aligned the two communities. This time as victims of prejudice, bigotry, racism and as a result for many, poverty. In the mid 20th century the phrase "No Irish, No Blacks, No Dogs" became a popular sentiment. As England was the epicentre for commerce, the majority of Caribbean's who came to the UK flocked to the industrial cities there but a select few chose the Emerald isle.

The legacy of this lives on today and across Ireland in both Northern Ireland and the Republic of Ireland Caribbean food can be found in small pockets. Places like Wendy McGuire's Windrush Island Cafe in Northern Ireland's capital of Belfast paved the way to introduce Caribbean favourites to the region before it unfortunately closed. In Ireland main, to the south in the city of Waterford, **Manna's Afro Caribbean Takeaway** taps into the West African heritage of the Caribbean serving up equal amounts of jollof rice to jerk chicken. Like most places however, the main action is in the capital with events, pop-ups and parties providing more opportunity for upstart food ventures. Here, in Dublin the food emerging from **Ruby Tuesday's Soul Food** has caused a flavour raucous. Their Jam-packed dishes of flavour including curry goat, jerk burgers and plantain salsa have gone a long ways to making Afro-Caribbean food a known entity in the city. Furthermore, with her special jerk sauce recipe Tuesday's claim the secret to the "best tasting chicken wings in Dublin."

Simultaneous to this, Nick Reynolds, **Lil Portie** has taken Dublin by storm wherever it pops-up. Nick fuses his own Jamaican heritage with an Irish upbringing as well as a love for South America into all his food. This is wonderfully illustrated in his vegan jerk jackfruit patacones and Cuban pork shoulder tacos with orange mojo. Naturally, the Jamaican classics like jerk chicken are all done amazingly with Reynold's distinctive flair. If you can't make it to one of his outposts, fortunately he shares various homely Caribbean recipes for you to try at home.

Wales

While the emergence of African and Afro-Caribbean communities in the UK are usually associated with the Windrush generation of the mid 20th century and after, Wales is a useful case study to examine a presence long before this. In the 17th century, Wales, like Ireland, had many of its citizens serve British leader Oliver Cromwell's armies against rival colonial powers in the Caribbean. As such, in the process the relationship between the two regions began.

According to records and archives, people from the Caribbean islands have been migrating to the UK since the 1670s, with many living in Cardiff's Tiger Bay area that covered Butetown and Cardiff Docks since the 1880s. In the midst of the transatlantic slave trade in the 18th century, many Afro-Caribbean people were brought over to Cardiff by planters, military or naval officers, serving as slaves and domestic servants for wealthy Welsh and British families.

In the early 1900s, many migrants introduced their cultural traditions and heritages to Cardiff and Caribbean individuals and descendants could be found throughout the country. This was not without friction and in 1919 there had been race riots in Tiger Bay, sparked by high unemployment and racial tensions. It was after the World Wars in the 1940s that Cardiff received another mass migration of people from the Caribbean that arguably birthed the community seen today. Recordings tell that 493 people were transported from Jamaica to the Welsh capital city on the HMS Empire Windrush in 1948. With them this grew into a sizable community that transplanted their culture and norms in the country and this included their food. It is told that throughout the 1940s, Caribbean people would come together in Cardiff to socialise at a place called the Caribbean Café, which was located on 185a Bute Road.

Just a few miles from this today in the area of Cathays sits **Irie Shack** by Iftekhar Harris who sought to keep the Caribbean legacy alive in the city. The restaurant serves everything that might have been found at that same Caribbean Cafe from charcoal flamed jerk pit jerk chicken to bone filled marinated curried goat. However, the restaurant also looks to the present diversity of Cardiff lending the vivid Caribbean taste to the likes of halloumi and locally sourced king prawns. Not limited to the confines of their own restaurant, the crew can be found celebrating Caribbean culture at local fests like Newport's Color Clash.

About one hour to the west in Wales' second city of Newport, **Jamaican Jills** has been spreading the Jamaican love with its numerous vibrant outposts. Here, in addition to curry chicken or goat, the restaurant fuses Caribbean and Welsh eating with the likes of the lamb shanks or jacket potatoes that can be served as default or jerked with an array of island inspired extras. At the foot of the Brecon beacons mountain range in the humble town of Merthyr Tydfil, Michael Hamilton's **Caribbean Cariad** has been doing the same Caribbean food evangelism but fusing the menu with American style soul food classics of southern fried chicken and barbecue wings.

The last stop on this Welsh tour up to the north in Aberystwyth is **Mama Fay's** another family run eatery with over a decade logged of serving Caribbean food to the Welsh citizenry. Here, traditional jerk pork and chicken go hand in hand with pan fried sea bass and prawn linguine. Vegans are well looked after with the option to go conventionally Caribbean with the Ital coconut stew and vegetable curry or a brilliant modern route with the likes of the jerk spiced hummus with hand-made tortilla chips or crispy halloumi sticks served with a tantalising restaurant recipe sweet chili sauce.

INDEX

Smokey Jerkey
158 New Cross Rd, New Cross, London,
SE14 5BA

Kaieteur Kitchen
35-336 Elephant and Castle, London
SE1 6TB
Scheduled to move Autumn 2020

True Flavours
101 Acre Ln, Brixton, London, SW2 5TU

People's Choice
51c Chatsworth Road, Hackney, E5 0LH

JB's Soulfood & Jerk Chicken
27A Peckham High St, Peckham,
London SE15 5EB

Zionly Food Hall
Rye Lane Indoor Market, 41, 48 Rye Ln,
Peckham, London SE15 5BY
Caribbean Kitchen
67 Mare St, Hackney, London E8 4RG,
United Kingdom

Bokit'la
Montgomery Hall, 58 Kennington Oval,
Vauxhall, London SE11 5SW
Check web or social for info on stalls

Mama's Jerk
10 Morning Ln, Hackney, London E9
6NA
33 Deptford High St, Deptford, London
SE8 4NS
Unit 4 Wharf Kitchen, Jubilee Place,
Canary Wharf, London E14 5NY

Jamaica Patty Co
26 New Row, London, WC2N 4LA

Eat of Eden
76 Shepherds Bush Rd, Hammersmith,
London W6 7PH

Ascot Parade, 6, Clapham Park Rd
SW4 7EY

House 32, 1 Goldcrest, 64 Lee High Rd,
London SE13 5FH

Unit 4, Brixton Village, Coldharbour Ln,
Brixton, London SW9 8PR

The Globe
103 Talbot Rd, Notting Hill, London,
W11 2AT

Hi-Lo Jamaican Eating House
68-70 Cowley Rd, Oxford, OX4 1JB

Plantation Inn
www.plantation-inn.co.uk Catering Only

Troy Bar
10 Hoxton St, Hackney, London N1 6NG

The Honeypot
9 Upper Brockley Rd, London, SE4 1SY

Jamaican Ways
107 Hartley Rd, Nottingham, NG7 3AQ

Dons Hut
840 Garratt Ln, Tooting, London,
SW17 0NA

Coconut Kitchen
456 Hornsey Rd, London, N19 4EE

Raggas
58 Smithdown Road Liverpool, L7 4JG

One Stop
17 High St, London, NW10 4NE

Rum Shack
657 - 659 Pollokshaws Rd, Glasgow
G41 2AB

Mullins Brasserie
6 Market Pl, Margate CT9 1EN

RivERlife
84 Dalry Rd, Edinburgh EH11 2AX

Fish, Wings & Ting
Brixton Village, 99 Coldharbour Ln,
Brixton, London SW9 8PR

Rhythm Kitchen
257 Hoe St, Walthamstow, London
E17 9PT

1F World Food Court, Westfield
Stratford City, Montfichet Rd, London
E20 1ES

Ayannas
2 Yabsley St, Poplar, London, E14 9RG

Rudies
2-10 Bethnal Green Rd, Hackney,
London E1 6GY
Borough Market, 8 Southwark St,
London SE1 1TL
Check web or social for Borough
market details
Brixton Address tbd

Pull Up Bar Café
14-16 Swan St, Manchester M4 5JN

Spiced Roots
64 Cowley Rd, Cowley, Oxford OX4 1JB

Three Little Birds
42 Battersea Rise, London SW11 1EE
412 Coldharbour Ln, Brixton, London
SW9 8LF

Buster Mantis
3-4 Resolution Way, London, SE8 4NT

Accurate as of August 2020

THANKS

My Entire Family, Grandma, Aunty Ann & Aunty Joy

Al 'Fingers' Newman, Alan Denney, Alice Hale, Anna Ginsburg, Anu Henriques,
Billy Jobling, Carin Nakanishi, Chlo Schwartz, Clem Bedos, Daisy Fletcher, Dan Bailey,
Duval Timothy, Elizabeth Wordsworth, Emmanuella Kwenortey, Esme Toler, Hakim Adi,
Hannah Hammond, Harry Mitchell, Ianthe Fry, Irene Agbotaen, Issy Timothy, Jack Gove,
Jacob Todd, Jahron Braithwaite, James Massiah, Jenny On, Joby Weston,
Jordan Ullman, Joshua Bernie, Katy Berry, Konrad Kay, Kitchen 54, Loren Platt,
Lydia Figes, Mali Nelson, Max Vallezadeh, Mickey Down, Miles Timothy, No Vacancy Inn,
Otis Clarke, Poppy MacInnes, Rabab Ahmad, Reverend Alex Thanni, Rivah Feseha,
Roxy Alexander, Saleem Dar, Shamayel Shalizi, Sharmadean Reid, Tara Rudd,
Tom Lazenby, Yemi Brown, Zandile Nkomo, Zack O'Toole, Zezi Ifore

@BELLY.FULL

Riaz Phillips is a London-based writer and photographer. Born in Hackney and raised in North London, he studied politics and economics at University in London followed by postgraduate study at the University of Oxford. After this he founded Tezeta Press.

Tezeta Press is an independent publishing company dedicated to celebrating and shining a much needed light on marginalized and under-represented ideas, history and culture.

Tezeta (ትዝታ) derives from the Amharic word, Tizita, a musical phrase in the East African language that connotes nostalgia and the idea of "Never forgetting."